O9-ABE-327

HEROES
of OHIO

23 True Tales
of Courage and Character

HEROES OF OHIO: (1) Baldemar Velasquez; (2) Oliver Hazard Perry; (3) Thomas Edison; (4) Toni Morrison; (5) Jane Edna Hunter; (6) Elizabeth Hauser; (7) Annie Oakley; (8) Neil Armstrong; (9) Rodger Young; (10) Mary Ann Bickerdyke; (11) Jesse Owens; (12) The Wright Family; (13) Simon Kenton; (14) Granville Woods; (15) Januarius MacGahan; (16) John Chapman; (17) Henry Heimlich; (18) Ulysses S. Grant; (19) Tecumseh; (20) Emma Gatewood; (21) Jacob Parrott; (22) Harriet Beecher Stowe; (23) John Parker.

HEROES of OHIO

23 True Tales
of Courage and Character

Rick Sowash
Storyteller of the Heartland

Illustrated by Marcia Muth

A James Hope book

Gabriel's Horn
Publishing Company

Bowling Green, Ohio

About the Cover and Frontispiece:

Marcia Muth, who lived in the Midwest for most of her life, is the artist. This work by her depicts the subjects of the tales told in *Heroes of Ohio*. See how many people you can name just by looking at the cover. The frontispiece (two pages before this one) will give you the answers when you get stuck.

Gabriel's Horn Publishing Co., Inc.
P.O. Box 141
Bowling Green, OH 43402
Editorial and business office: (419) 352-1338
FAX: (419) 352-1488
E-mail: gabriel@hornbooks.com
Orders only: 800/235-HORN (that's 4676)

Cover painting (and excerpts therefrom printed inside) by Marcia Muth, © 1998 by Gabriel's Horn Publishing Co., Inc. All rights reserved. All other inside illustrations used by permission.

Editorial contents of book © 1998 by Rick Sowash. All rights reserved. All other editorial, advertising and illustrative matter not otherwise credited are protected by © 1998, Gabriel's Horn Publishing Co. All rights reserved. The name and symbol of Gabriel's Horn Publishing Co., Inc., are legally protected trademarks and may not be used without permission.

No part of this book may be duplicated, transmitted or reproduced in any electronic or mechanical manner whatsoever—including with any photocopying, recording or information storage and retrieval system—without express written permission from the appropriate copyright owner and holder of rights to reproduction, Gabriel's Horn Publishing Co., Inc. Brief quotations may be embodied in critical articles, reviews and news reports. For information on any copyrighted material appearing in this book, write the publisher.

Manufactured in the United States of America.

08 07 06 05 04 03 02 01 00 99 98   15 14 13 12 11 10 9 8 7 6 5 4 3 2 1

Softcover: ISBN 0-911861-13-0
Hardcover: ISBN 0-911861-12-2

Heroes on the Web:

For news and the latest information about our heroes, get on the World Wide Web and click on <http://www.ourheroes.com>. To learn more about author Rick Sowash, go to <http://www.sowash.com>.

Publisher's Cataloging-in-Publication Data

Sowash, Rick, 1950—
    Heroes of Ohio: 23 true tales of courage and character / Rick Sowash ; illustrated by Marcia Muth.
    xii, 138 p. : ill. ; 24 cm.
    Includes index.
    ISBN 0-911861-12-2 : $19.95. – ISBN 0-911861-13-0 (pbk.) : $11.95.
Heroes—Ohio—Biography. 2. Ohio—Biography. 3. Courage.
1998
920.0771 [B]

Dedication

In memory of my grandfather, John Hoff.
I loved when he told me history stories.

———

And to my son, John Chapman Sowash.
He loves when I tell him history stories.

Let me tell you a tale—

the tale of a hero—twenty-three tales of people who were heroes
in twenty-three different ways. And all of them were from Ohio!

Some lived long ago and some are alive right now. They're from
different parts of the state and they are people of different colors,
religions and walks of life.

All had the guts and grit to do
great things.

Their stories have stirred me and
will stir you. Their stories will make
you think and make you grow. Their
stories might even make you want
to follow in their footsteps.

Let me tell you a tale...

Contents

Acknowledgements x

Introduction xi

───────────────── **PART I** ─────────────────
HEROES OF EARLY TIMES

Page 3 *Chapter 1*
John Chapman
The Best-Known Ohioan

Page 9 *Chapter 2*
Simon Kenton
The Frontiersman

Page 15 *Chapter 3*
Tecumseh
The Man Called Crouching Panther

Page 21 *Chapter 4*
Oliver Hazard Perry
He Met the Enemy

───────────────── **PART II** ─────────────────
HEROES OF OUR DARKEST TIMES

Page 27 *Chapter 5*
John Parker
Rescuer of Slaves

Page 33 *Chapter 6*
Harriet Beecher Stowe
One Cause of the Big War

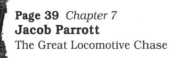

Page 39 *Chapter 7*
Jacob Parrott
The Great Locomotive Chase

Page 45 *Chapter 8*
Mary Ann Bickerdyke
Mother of the Battlefield

Page 51 *Chapter 9*
Ulysses S. Grant
Grant's Last Battle

PART III
HEROES OF INVENTION

Page 57 *Chapter 10*
Thomas Alva Edison
A Thousand Inventions

Page 63 *Chapter 11*
Granville Woods
The Black Edison

Page 69 *Chapter 12*
Orville, Katherine & Wilbur Wright
They Wanted to Fly

PART IV
HEROES OF CHANGE

Page 75 *Chapter 13*
Januarius MacGahan
Liberator of Bulgaria

Page 81 *Chapter 14*
Annie Oakley
Little Sure Shot

Page 87 *Chapter 15*
Jane Edna Hunter
A Nickel and a Prayer

Page 93 *Chapter 16*
Elizabeth Hauser
Parade in the Rain

PART V

HEROES OF OUR GRANDPARENTS

Page 99 *Chapter 17*
Jesse Owens
He Beat the Nazis

Page 105 *Chapter 18*
Rodger Young
Little Man, Big Hero

Page 111 *Chapter 19*
Emma Gatewood
More Head than Heels

PART VI

HEROES OF OUR OWN TIMES

Page 117 *Chapter 20*
Neil Armstrong
One Small Step

Page 123 *Chapter 21*
Toni Morrison
Trailblazer with a Pen

Page 129 *Chapter 22*
Baldemar Velazquez
"God Belongs to Me, Too!"

Page 135 *Chapter 23*
Henry Heimlich M.D.
The Maneuver Man

Index 141
The Author 143
The Artist and the Designer 144

Acknowledgements

By the Author

Great thanks are due to my editor, Jim Bissland of Gabriel's Horn Publishing, for his thoughtful and tactful guidance. I could not have written this book without him.

Thanks, too, to my two beloved proofreaders: Ann Ackerman, who was my high school English teacher, and her daughter, my wife of 25+ years, Jo Anna Ackerman Sowash.

By the Publisher

It is impossible to recall all the people who have helped in various ways to make this book possible. However, the following cannot go unnamed:

Ray Crain Mike Major, Dave Martin, Joe Murray, Richard E. Leibel Jr., Jeanne Palermo, Lana Eisenbraun, Brian B. King, Loretta Jones, the staff of FLOC, Vicki Roberts, Amy Dawson, Marcia Brennan, Vernon Will, Eric Davis, Julie Shaw, Barb Vogel, Ann Sindelar, Chris Grasso, and especially Kim Sautter.

Special appreciation is due to Paul Obringer, who not only designed these pages but set the type and processed the art.

Introduction

By Rick Sowash

My idea of a hero has changed over the years. My grandfather used his wonderful storytelling skills to bring to life for me the great heroes of the past. They had courage and character. The things they did were grand, earth-shaking, awesome. I wanted to be like them. But I didn't see how a kid could ever be that kind of hero.

Later I realized that my grandfather was a hero. He was never famous but he faced some big challenges and did some pretty big things in his own small way.

Still later, I began to see that there are heroes all around us. Our neighbors, our classmates, our friends. They aren't featured on TV and no one writes books about them, but they are heroes just the same. Why? Because they show courage and character.

Neighbors who see another neighbor in need and get to work on the problem. Drivers who stop to help change a stranger's flat tire or rescue someone who has run out of gas. The old man who stiffly stoops over to pick up a little litter every time he walks his dog. The single mom who works so hard to provide for and care for her children that she has almost no time left for herself.

Teachers are great heroes. It takes courage and character to give a whole year to help one small group of kids learn things they need to know.

Kids themselves can be heroes. When they protect another kid against a bully. When they turn down cigarettes, alcohol or drugs, even when they know other kids will put them down because of it. When they won't put down other kids—not for being different from themselves, not for anything. When they do what's honest instead of what's easy.

Heroes aren't forced to do what they do. They've got the courage to face a challenge, even when they don't have to. They've got the character to volunteer. And what they do helps other people. In other words, what heroes do is NOT EASY, NOT REQUIRED, AND NOT SELFISH.

Heroes hold our world together. Once you understand this, you see how we all depend on each other.

Some heroes are giants, like the ones in this book. They changed the world; most became famous. There can only be a few such heroes. But all of us can be heroes in some way almost every day. It takes courage and character. Ordinary people like you and me have these qualities. They're like muscles. The more you use them, the stronger they become. We just need to be reminded to put them to work.

I've always loved hearing, reading and telling hero stories. In fact, I collect such stories. We all do. We collect them into our memory, the way people collect coins or stamps or rocks or books signed by the author.

We need stories of heroes, both famous and unknown. Their stories remind us to try to be like them, to put courage and character to work in our own lives.

Maybe there can be more books like this one. Maybe you can help write them. Look around you. Notice the heroes. Look for stories of courage and character in your community, your school, your circle of friends. I'd like to hear you tell their stories. Maybe some of them— maybe your own story—could be in my collection. And maybe some of the heroes I tell you about in this book will become part of your collection, will inspire you, will remind you to grab every chance you have to be a hero.

HEROES *of* OHIO

23 True Tales of Courage and Character

The Best-Known Ohioan:

John Chapman
1774-1845

Children aren't happy all the time. Some are very unhappy much of the time. Yet some of these – John Chapman, for one – grow up and bring happiness to many others.

Young "Johnny Appleseed"
(upper left) planted apple trees throughout
Ohio. When he warned settlers of an Indian
attack, they took refuge in a blockhouse,
which still stands in Mansfield.

Little John Chapman was the apple of his mother's eye. Newborn babies usually are.

This baby had arrived in the Chapmans' Leominster, Massachusetts, home in late September, 1774. That time of year the sweet smell of apples filled every home. People baked apple pies. They made apple butter to spread on warm, fresh-baked bread on the cold winter mornings to come. They hung apples from their ceilings to dry— dried apples would stay fresh for months. They squeezed apples to make cider from the juice. They drank some of the cider. The rest they made into vinegar. Vegetables soaking in apple vinegar do not spoil.

In those days people needed apples much more than we do today. They could not live without them.

Tiny little newborn Johnny looked a lot like an apple himself. His head wasn't much bigger than an apple. He was red and plump and juicy. His mother said he looked good enough to eat!

When she died two years later, her last thoughts must have been about Johnny. What would become of him? His father was far away, fighting the British in the Revolutionary War. The neighbors buried her and took Johnny to live with them.

Not for long. His father returned from the fighting. But the war was not over. Why had he come back so soon? Didn't General Washington need every man?

Then people found out. Johnny's father had been kicked out of the army. There had been some kind of trouble. Nathaniel Chapman would say nothing about it. People never found out much.

The former soldier soon married again. In the next ten years, ten brothers and sisters came along. The Chapman house was small and noisy. The only peace and quiet Johnny could find was outside among the apple trees or far off in the woods. He loved to sit as still as he could and watch the animals come near. They seemed to like him. They didn't laugh or make mean jokes about his father.

The Fourth of July was the worst day of the year for Johnny. On that day the men who had served with General Washington all marched in a parade. Their wives and children stood by and cheered.

But Johnny's father stayed out of sight on the Fourth of July. He had been kicked out of the army, so he was not welcome to march with the other men. Johnny felt his cheeks burn as red as apples. He hid among the apple trees or with his animal friends in the woods.

As soon as he was old enough, he left the village, never to return.

Some say he went to sea and became a sailor. They say that's why he went barefoot the rest of his life. Sailors always went barefoot in those days. They say that's where he learned that apples kept illness away. Sailors ate fruit to stay healthy.

Ten years later Johnny came to Pittsburgh, Pennsylvania. He bought a canoe, a few supplies and several sacks of apple seeds. He bought a little land not far from Pittsburgh and soon had apple trees growing there. But he didn't stay there for long. He was eager to move west into Ohio. One winter day he decided to go as far west as he could before spring came.

People saw Johnny canoeing down the Ohio River. His paddle dipped and swung and dipped again in the icy water. When night came, other travelers tied their boats to the shore and made camp. Not Johnny. He just pulled his canoe onto a chunk of ice. Then he curled up among his sacks of apple seeds and went to sleep. All night long the chunk of ice floated down the river. Most people would have been afraid. What if the chunk of ice hit a rock and tipped over? But Johnny was in a hurry. In the morning Johnny stretched himself and ate a little cornbread. Then he shoved his canoe off the ice and dipped and swung his paddle all day long.

P eople wondered. What was the hurry? There was nothing in Ohio. The great dark forest had stood there, silent and still, for 100,000 years. What was there that anyone would want to hurry?

Johnny had good reasons for hurrying. People were heading west. He knew that there would soon be hundreds of people living in Ohio, then thousands. They needed apples — they could not live without them. It takes time for seeds to grow into saplings, and saplings into trees, and trees to bear fruit. And there wasn't much time left.

Johnny looked over the land and studied where the streams came together. He knew that was where villages would be built. He planted his seeds near these places. He meant to supply the new villagers with all the apples they would need.

People said Ohio was an empty place. But it wasn't. There were already plenty of people living there when Johnny arrived. Red people. Many of Ohio's newly arriving people feared and hated the red people who were already here. The red people came to fear and hate the new people in turn.

Johnny didn't hate or fear anybody or anything. He had no time or energy for hating and fearing. Johnny only wanted to plant and care for apple trees.

The red people saw how much Johnny cared for his little trees. They thought he was crazy. Not that they minded. They respected crazy people. They thought crazy people knew things and felt what other people couldn't know or feel. They thought crazy people were magical.

To tell the truth, the newly arrived people also thought Johnny was a little crazy. In their rough talk about him, some said he was "tetched." This was their way of saying he was "touched on the head," that God had touched him and made him different from others.

He certainly was different. He had no wife and didn't seem to want one. He loved children but had none of his own. He wore strange hats and raggedy clothes and went barefoot all year long. He had no real home. He planted thousands of apple trees, but he owned almost no land. He could recite Bible verses for hours at a time. When he talked about God, a strange look came into his eyes.

Still, people liked him. Especially red people and new people. Johnny probably figured that if the red people and the new people both liked him, then they would also like each other.

Sadly, that was not true. The red people wanted to stop the new people from coming into Ohio and claiming their land. And the British still hoped to defeat America. Soon the red people and the British joined together to fight the Americans.

The War of 1812 came to the forests and farms of the new state of Ohio. Arrows and tomahawks flew. Rifles flashed in the darkness of the forest. Flames rose from the farmhouses. The screams of attacking warriors were answered by the cries of the wounded and dying.

Johnny had always carried news to the settlers. News of spring planting and fall harvest. News of the names of newly arriving people. News of newlyweds. News of newborn babies, new villages and the names people gave them.

Now his news was dark and terrible. While others hid inside quickly built forts, Johnny still moved freely about. He wasn't afraid for himself. Red people still liked him. But everywhere he heard tales of attacks, scalpings and massacres.

He found sixty settlers huddled together in the little blockhouse at a new village called Mansfield. Over 400 red warriors were nearby. Everyone expected an attack. There were American soldiers at Mt. Vernon, thirty miles away. If they came, they could rescue the settlers. But the soldiers had to be told. Who would make the risky run to Mt. Vernon?

Johnny would, that's who. He ran the thirty miles alone. He returned with the soldiers. He saved Mansfield, and Mansfielders love his name to this day.

The war ended. The Americans won. The red-coated British and most of Ohio's red people were driven out forever.

Mansfielders wanted Johnny to make his home among them. But not even the grateful love of the growing town was enough to make Johnny settle in one place. He had work to do. He went west into Indiana. Right up to the end of his life, he planted his apple seeds. New people kept coming, more than ever, and they needed apples.

He was born in Massachusetts and was buried in Indiana, but Johnny is Ohio's best-known hero. Go to any school in America. Ask the kids to raise their hands if they've heard of certain Ohio heroes. Try Edison, Grant, the Wright Brothers, Annie Oakley, Tecumseh, Neil Armstrong. With each name, a few hands may go up.

But shout out the name of Johnny Appleseed, and you'll see every hand held high.

To learn more...

Johnny Appleseed is one of America's most cherished folk figures, but there are surprisingly few traces of him in Ohio. That's why the author of this book has long believed Ohio needs a national monument to Johnny.

The blockhouse mentioned in the story still stands in Mansfield. That city also has a junior high school and a Boy Scout council named in Johnny's honor.

John Chapman began planting apple trees in Indiana in the 1830s. He happened to be in Fort Wayne when death overtook him. That city later erected a monument in his memory.

Among the many books about Johnny is Steven Kellogg's *Johnny Appleseed* (New York: William Morrow, 1988). See also *The Johnny Appleseed Homepage* at <http:// www.msc.cornell.edu/%7eweeds/SchoolPages/Appleseed/welcome.html>.

The Frontiersman:

Simon Kenton

1755-1836

Heroes must sometimes face opponents...foes and even friends with whom they don't agree. But opponents can be treated with respect. Heroes fight hard. They also fight fair.

Simon Kenton's
statue (including his faithful dog)
marks his grave in Urbana. Kenton's many
acts of courage included saving Daniel Boone
from the Indians in Kentucky.

Old Simon Kenton stood stock still. He was half-hidden in the thick shade at the edge of the Urbana militia camp. But he was near enough to catch every word of the troublemaker's blurred and bawling speech.

"We come here fer jus' one reason—to kill Injuns! Am I right, boys?"

A round of shouts rose from the buckskinned militiamen.

"We dinnah come here," the speaker went on, "jus' fer marchin' up and down, an' paradin' back and forth, an' takin' orders from a lot uh hifalutin', fan-tailed, ring-necked, fancy-pants officers what don't know a wild turkey from a guinea hen—now DID we, boys?"

"No!" the men roared.

"Well, then, whuh-dar we waitin' fer? We KNOW they're out there— a tidy passel of 'em— and not an hour's walk from where we're standin': a whole village of savages, prob'ly breedin' like rats ev'ry second we stand here. Breedin' faster 'n mosquitoes, churnin' out filthy redskinned runts by the hour—which is why we got to kill ALL of 'em, not jus' the grown men. We got to kill 'em ALL! An' we got to do it NOW before these here officers come up with another one of them fool peace treaties."

He jumped to his feet and waved his flintlock rifle in the air. "Who's comin' with me?" he shouted. He spun dizzily on his heel and started out.

The men loosed their loudest roar yet and fell in behind him.

But their leader had only reached the edge of the forest when he jerked to a halt. A tall, grim figure stepped from behind a tree and blocked the way. Every militiaman knew him at once. There was no more famous Indian-fighter on the Ohio frontier than Simon Kenton.

"And where might you be going?" Kenton asked, quietly.

"You heard," several of the men answered.

"Well, now, I did hear what sounded like a lot of big talk," Kenton said. He cast his eye over the loud-mouthed leader of the group. "But I'm not real certain that I heard right. I thought I heard somethin' about attackin' Injuns."

"You heard right enough," the leader growled. "Stand aside."

Kenton stood firm, hands on his hips. He caught the smell of whiskey on the man's breath. "So you come to fight Injuns," he said after a time. His voice was low, but every man there could hear what he said. His lips closed in a thin, strong line and his long hair bobbed as he nodded.

"You'll be gettin' your chance, and before long, too. You'll be fightin' Injuns soon enough, and British soldiers, too. The best army in the world. Trained men who can hold a line together under cannon fire, thousands of such men, wearin' the prettiest red coats you'll ever see. Men who can TAKE ORDERS." Kenton pushed these last two words a little as he said them. Then he stared hard, right into the militiamen's eyes. Some dropped their eyes and looked away. They felt ashamed.

Kenton's voice got even softer. "There's a word for what you're thinking of doing," he said. *"Mutiny."*

"Mutiny?" their leader yelled. He tried to force out a laugh. "Pah! We don't hafta listen tuh this. Now get outa the way, Kenton. If you don't have it in your belly to join us, you can stay back here and jaw away the time with yer fancy officer friends."

A flicker of anger flashed over Kenton's old face. Nearing sixty, his frown was full of deep lines. The men had seen his wrinkled smile far more often.

"If militia men attack without orders?" he asked. "If they attack a village of peaceful men, women and children, who settled there with the promise they would be left alone? Then, yes, that's mutiny, plain and simple. Low, cowardly mutiny!"

This brought a rumble of angry murmurs from the men, but none of them spoke clearly or directly to Kenton. They knew his story. They knew he'd fled his boyhood home back in Virginia, fearing he'd killed a neighbor in a fight over a woman. They knew he'd lost his first wife. They knew his heartbreak when his little daughter died and when his grown son disappeared. Simon Kenton was a man who knew what it meant to lose women and children.

He seemed a strange one to talk about showing respect for orders. He'd been caught on the wrong side of the law more than once. Yet here he was, standing up for law and order—and on the side of the Indians!

"What do YOU know about Indians?" he asked. "Which of you knows a half, or a tenth, or even a hundredth part of what I know about them?"

The men were silent now.

"I was out here forty years ago, when I could count on one hand the number of white men in Ohio. I've looked Tecumseh in the eye. I was with Daniel Boone in Kentucky, and I saved his life more than once. There's not a man among you who's worked longer or fought harder to make the state of Ohio what it is today."

His voice had risen to a shout. Now it was low again. "I've spilled more Indian blood than all the blood that flows in all the bodies of all the men of this whole militia!" His eyes wheeled about, staring for a split-second into the eyes of every man who would still look at him.

He whispered, "And I've known Indians at their worst."

Every man there had heard the terrible stories of the times Kenton had been captured and tortured. He had been made to "run the gauntlet" again and again, whipped and beaten as he sprinted between a double column of lashing, clubbing braves. He'd been staked to the ground for days on end. He'd escaped and been recaptured to face the full fury of his enemies. And the only reason he was saved was because that no-good rascal Simon Girty–of all people!–had begged the Indians to spare the life of his onetime friend.

The drunken leader found his voice again. "These Injuns is savages, Kenton, like all the rest. You know it jus' as well as we do."

"They are not," Kenton said, simple and firm. "What I DO know, just as well as you, is that only a pack of low, dirty cowards would kill peaceful people."

A wave of anger passed through the crowd. "Peaceful!" some hissed. It was not a word they used in talking about Indians. Kenton went on. Now he coaxed the men in a voice that seemed warm and wise.

"You are not cowards. You are soldiers. You have promised to do your duty. Your duty is to follow orders. And you know, every one of you, that your orders are to stay in this camp until the time comes to march off together. And not to attack until you are told to attack."

The leader's red face seemed to get darker as Kenton spoke. Now his face was twisted with rage, his lips trembling.

"You got no call to preach to us about what's our duty and what ain't," he snarled. "Our duty's to kill Injuns. That's what we aim to do."

The man reached for his tomahawk. A few others squeezed their knife-handles or shifted their rifles. "I don't know what kinda crazy Injun-lovin' ideas has got into your head! But I'm tellin' you now, Kenton, and fer the las' time, if you ain't comin' along, then you kin STAND ASIDE!"

Kenton's rifle seemed almost to jump into his hands from where it had been leaning, out of sight, behind a nearby tree. He stuck the end of the barrel right into the leader's ugly face.

"I'll come along," Kenton said slowly. He spoke through his teeth. The corners of his hooded eyes twitched strangely, and a chilling grin spread across his weathered features.

"And I will shoot dead the first man who lays a hand on any Injun in that village. And I'll take down as many of the rest of you as I can. And after I am brought down, those of you who still have a mind to pay a visit to that village will have to step wide as you pass over my dead body. And you'll have to do some hard thinking later on, when you come tell just why it was that you had to kill old Simon Kenton."

There was a long, long wait. Everyone stood frozen in place, waiting to see what would happen next. Finally some of the men in the rear of the party turned and headed back to the militia camp. Others soon followed and the group melted away. The leader rolled his eyes in disgust, spat and laughed loudly, as if it had all been a good joke. At long last he turned, too.

Old Simon Kenton stood alone once again at the edge of the forest.

To learn more...

Simon Kenton, Frontiersman, is the title of an illustrated web site which will also tell you about the modern descendants of Simon Kenton and family events: <http://www.webpub.com/~jhagee/kenton.html>.

The story of Simon Kenton is wonderfully recounted in *Simon Kenton: The Great Frontiersman* and other books by Ray Crain (Main Graphics, 1992) and in many histories of the state. Hard to find, but filled with detail and rare pictures—even a copy of Simon Kenton's first known signature!—is *Simon Kenton: His Life and Period, 1755-1836* (Garden City: Doubleday, Doran, 1930), by Edna Kenton.

The city of Kenton in Hardin County is named for our hero, of course. In 1998 State Route 68 from Ripley to Kenton was named "The Simon Kenton Highway." There is a statue of Kenton at his grave in a cemetery in Urbana. The city of Springfield got its name from Simon Kenton's wife. She called the area that because of the many springs bubbling up from the meadows. A natural wet meadow like those in Kenton's time can still be found in Buck Creek State Park near here.

3

The Man Called Crouching Panther:

Tecumseh
1768-1813

The fight of the few against the many always inspires us. Badly outnumbered, Tecumseh led his people's defense against invasion. Probably he knew he would fail. We can admire him for trying.

Tecumseh,
a great Indian leader,
tried to negotiate with the white men
before fighting to defend his people.
His story is re-told (photo) in
an outdoor drama staged every
summer in Chillicothe.

he white flag of truce trembled, yet there wasn't a wisp of wind. It trembled because the soldier who held it was trembling. Fear shook him. Fear twisted down the corners of his mouth. His voice was high and strained.

He stood alone and without a weapon in the center of a vast and silent crowd of angry faces. Red faces with dark, frowning eyes. Strong arms and bare chests glistened in the orange light of a blazing campfire. Weird shadows fell away all about them.

The red leader Tecumseh looked at the soldier with scorn. Weak, he thought. Alone, these whites are weak. When one warrior fights one soldier, the warrior wins. Always. But he knew that there were many, many more whites than warriors.

This one soldier had come alone to bring Tecumseh a message. The white leader—General William Henry Harrison, governor of the Territory—was asking Tecumseh to come to his house in Vincennes.

Tecumseh did not say he would come. He would not deal with messengers. A warrior would give his answer later. Instead he cut to the point.

"The Great Spirit gave this land to his red children," he said in the deep and powerful voice his warriors loved so well. Their feathers quivered as the warriors nodded. "He placed the whites on the other side of the big water. The Great Spirit ordered us to come here, and here we will stay."

"Yes, sir," the soldier was saying, talking too fast. "Yes, sir, Mister...Mister Tecumseh." How is such a leader called? General? Chief? The soldier felt like a fool. A very scared fool.

Tecumseh turned away. The soldier felt strong hands grab his arms. He thought that now he would die. Instead he was swiftly taken to the edge of the gathering place. One warrior said to him, "Tecumseh will come." Then he was alone. He ran like a rabbit.

A few days later four hundred Shawnee warriors came down the Wabash River in eighty canoes. Their faces and bodies were painted brightly for war. Their paddles flashed in the sunlight. The soldiers watched them from the little log fort at Vincennes. Suddenly it seemed as flimsy as a house of cards.

They had all heard of Tecumseh, the leader of the Ohio Shawnees and of many other tribes as well. Some said he commanded every red warrior there was, from Florida to Canada, from the Ohio Valley to the Great Plains. They said he could muster them all into one mighty army. They said that if he ever did, all the raids and battles of the last fifty years would be nothing next to the massacre to come. Any whites who were not killed would be forced back east, forever.

Then a new nation of red peoples, led by Tecumseh, would demand—and get!—the same respect America showed England or France.

The soldiers sent a runner to General Harrison with the news that Tecumseh had come and brought a terrifying army with him.

Harrison wiped his forehead. Tecumseh! He had invited him to Vincennes to show him that he dare not take on the United States of America. Now here he was, making camp with his army just outside the town, acting as if it was his land. Harrison sent word for Tecumseh to meet him at the Governor's House the next morning.

Harrison did not sleep well that night. He was not scared. Maybe he was troubled. Deep in his heart, maybe Harrison had half a notion that Tecumseh was right. This land really did belong to the red people. White Americans were stealing it.

Bah! Something else in Harrison shouted back. Seven million Americans were crowding the East Coast. They were not going to be stopped by scattered tribes of red savages, only a hundred thousand at most. Americans were surging over the mountains, coming on strong with rifles, axes and plows. The country was going to stretch "from sea to shining sea." Not even the great Tecumseh could hold it back. And yet....

The next morning Harrison stood before his fine house. At his side were other generals in fancy dress uniforms and judges in black robes. Some red chiefs were also there. They were ones who had signed the new treaty selling more land to the whites.

Harrison meant to show Tecumseh his power, his house, his men. He meant to show him that the red people must give up their lands and move further west.

There was no mistaking Tecumseh. Here he came, tall and powerful. His deerskins swung gracefully about him as he strode near. He made the white men's robes and uniforms seem a foolish way to dress. One soldier later called Tecumseh "one of the finest looking men I ever saw—about six feet high, straight, with large, fine features...a daring, bold-looking fellow."

There were solemn greetings. Harrison pointed to his house where tables and chairs were ready. Tecumseh folded his arms and said, "We hold council in the open air." He told Harrison that chairs were for white men. "The earth is my mother," he said. "I will rest in her lap." He sat down on the grass and his warriors did likewise. The white men were left to stand.

T ecumseh began to speak. His skill was famous. He told the shameful story of the white people's treatment of the red.

"The white men are not friends. Nothing will satisfy them but the whole of our hunting grounds, from the rising to the setting sun. The white men do not think the red men good enough to live....

"Once we had freedom without bounds. We had no riches, we had no wants. How is it now? Are we not stripped day by day of our freedom?"

Americans broke their promises, he said. They pushed ever west. They made farms where forests had stood. They made new treaties with weak tribes, he said, with a black look at the chiefs who stood with Harrison.

The recent treaty meant nothing, he said. His voice began to rise. "We now claim a common right to the land...It belongs to all! No tribe has the right to sell, not even to each other, and never to strangers!"

Tecumseh's deep voice boomed as everyone's eyes grew wide. "Sell a country!" Tecumseh cried. "Why not sell the air, the great sea, the earth? Did not the Great Spirit make them all for the use of his children?"

Silence fell on the crowd. Tecumseh had stopped speaking. Harrison tried to fall back on the speech he had ready.

"The United States has been fair with the tribes," he began. "We have treaties signed by chiefs."

Tecumseh shot to his feet. "We will kill those chiefs!" he shouted.

Harrison's chiefs reached for their weapons, but Tecumseh's tomahawk had already flashed from his belt. Harrison jumped in front of him. "You are all great chiefs!" he cried out. "And we have been fair. These chief's people are happy–"

"Liar!" Tecumseh roared and waved his tomahawk inches from Harrison's head. The General's sword rang as he pulled it out. Everyone jumped. The soldiers cocked their rifles. The warriors clenched their knives and tomahawks. Tecumseh himself hunched forward like a panther, ready to attack.

Harrison suddenly recalled something he had heard. "Crouching Panther" was one meaning of the name "Tecumseh." Now he saw why.

The two leaders slowly lowered their weapons. The meeting was over. There could be no peace.

In the War of 1812 Tecumseh and his followers joined forces with the British. He believed that if Great Britain won that war, his red people's nation would be honored. But then America's Oliver Hazard Perry beat the British Navy at the Battle of Lake Erie. Shortly after, Harrison's army attacked the British redcoats and Tecumseh's red warriors.

The British fell back and left the red warriors to fight on alone. All through the battle the Americans heard the red leader "yelling like a tiger," as one later recalled. Come sundown, Tecumseh's enemies had won. And he was dead.

Tecumseh's dream of a red people's nation died with him. And yet, he left something behind, after all. In the minds of thoughtful Americans, Tecumseh planted a seed of doubt, a shadow of guilt, a lingering hint that "we" have not always been "the good guys."

Look at a map of our state. Read the red people's names that flow across it. Names of rivers, counties and towns. Even the very word "Ohio." Now look closer. A face is watching you from behind the map. A face with dark, angry eyes. The face speaks. It says, "This land was ours. You were wrong to steal it. And we were right to defend it, even if we lost in the end."

It is the face Harrison saw at Vincennes.

It is the face of Tecumseh.

To learn more...

Read the story of Tecumseh in Zachary Kent's book, *Tecumseh* (Children's Press, 1992). For older readers, there are two dramatic (and sometimes dramatized) tellings: *A Sorrow in Our Heart*, by Allan W. Eckert (Smithmark, 1994) and *Panther in the Sky* by James Alexander Thorn (Del Ray, 1991).

Thanks to Eckert's book, the Indian leader's story comes alive in *Tecumseh!*, an outdoor historical drama performed each summer near Chillicothe. For information, write *Tecumseh!*, Box 73, Chillicothe, OH 45601. Ohio is rich in Indian artifacts and historic sites; there are too many to list here. However, one good starting point is the Ohio Historical Center, at the junction of I-71 and 17th Avenue in Columbus, with year-round exhibits. Tel. (614) 297-2300. The Sunwatch Prehistoric Archaelogical Park and Indian Village, on I-75 near Dayton, is open spring through fall; tel. (937) 268-8199. The Fort Ancient State Memorial in Oregonia is a fascinating museum and archaelogical site; tel. (513) 932-4421.

Wonderful resources can be found on the Smithsonian Institute's Web site for its National Museum of the American Indian:< http://www.si.edu/nmai>.

He Met the Enemy:

Oliver Hazard Perry
1785-1819

Oliver Hazard Perry was a leader. He was clear-sighted, persistent, determined and brave. He'd better have been. He was taking on the navy of the most powerful nation on earth.

Oliver Hazard Perry
simply moved to another ship,
the *Niagara*, and kept fighting after
the British sank his first one.
Repaired and restored, the *Niagara*
(photo) still sails Lake Erie.

ommodore Oliver Hazard Perry, 28-year-old commander of the American fleet on Lake Erie, swept his eyes over his ships one last time. He had to be sure that everything was ready for the battle that was—at last!—at hand.

For months he had pushed himself, pushed his men, demanding their utmost. It had taken every man and all the oxen Perry could find to tug five ships up Lake Erie to Buffalo. The men had arrived worn out. To make things worse, Perry and many of his men caught an illness called "lake fever."

Even so, they began right away to cut trees for more ships. They had to build five more. Perry's carpenters grumbled about the green lumber, but there was nothing else. The ships had to last only long enough to meet and defeat the enemy, then carry General William Henry Harrison's army to Canada. It was the War of 1812. A young United States of America was fighting the British again. If General Harrison could get to Canada and beat the British and Indian forces there, a big part of the war would be won.

Perry had pressed Harrison for more men, more men! Most of all he needed good sailors, but he would take any men he could get. General Harrison sent him all the Kentucky mountain boys he could spare.

That whole spring and summer of 1813, Perry's men kept on building ships. And all that time Perry expected the British to attack.

But the British did not attack.

In those days Britain ruled the waves. The Americans were building ships? So what! No British admiral need fear a tiny fleet of green ships manned by green crews.

But the British should have been more careful. Not all of Perry's men were so green. Some, like Perry, were Rhode Islanders who had built ships all their lives. There were men in Perry's force who had fought bravely in other battles. Perhaps the British had forgotten that as their fleet finally sailed toward battle. They would meet the Americans near South Bass Island in Lake Erie. It was September 10, 1813.

Perry and his men watched the British fleet draw near. It was quite a sight. Two ships, two brigs, a schooner and a sloop, they moved swiftly across the blue waters, their fresh paint shining, red ensigns flying, white sails bellying forth. Their goal was a terrible one: to help wipe out the United States of America. It would be a sweet revenge for America's winning the Revolutionary War against the British. The British thought it would be easy. This day, however, Perry planned to humble them.

His own fleet was a little bigger than the British but most of his ships were smaller than theirs. Also, his cannon could not fire as far as the British could. The Americans would have to get close to the British to have any hope of victory. So each American captain had his orders: Seek out the ship assigned to you, lay close along her side—and pound 'er!

Perry was on the *Lawrence*, which he had named for a friend. The friend had been killed in action not long before, battling the British. Captain Lawrence's dying words to his men were, "Don't give up the ship!" Perry had made Lawrence's last order the motto of his own ship. From its highest mast, flying just under the American flag, a blue flag flapped in the wind. On it, in big white letters, were the words: "Don't give up the ship!"

The British were nearer now, perhaps a mile off. Perry could see their marines swarming in the masts, rifles ready. He could see their gunners peering from the gunports, the sailors wetting the layer of sand spread on the decks to prevent fire. Then the faint sound of a distant bugle reached his ears from the British ship *Detroit.*

A puff of white smoke caught his eye. A moment later he heard the sharp report of a cannon, followed by a nearby splash. The *Detroit* had fired the first shot!

Nothing more happened for five long minutes. The British and American ships drew nearer and nearer. The *Detroit* fired again and this shot crashed into the *Lawrence* with a shuddering thud.

Perry gave orders to get close to the British as fast as possible. He knew their big guns outnumbered his own. His ships must close in quickly before the British cut them apart.

Perry's other large ship, the *Niagara,* had been just behind the *Lawrence.* Its captain's name was Elliott. Instead of keeping up with Perry as he should have, Elliott held back. But the *Lawrence* kept sailing toward the *Detroit* with such boldness that the British feared the Americans meant to board her. To prevent that, every one of the British ships started firing at the *Lawrence.*

Perry's ship took a fearsome pounding. Masts, sails and rigging fell, splinters flew, men shrieked, blood spread out in circles of crimson mud on the decks. For more than two hours the *Lawrence* fought on in a hail of enemy fire. Still the *Niagara* did not come to her aid. The *Lawrence* was badly outgunned. One by one, her cannons fell silent as the sharpshooting rifles of the British picked off the American sailors.

Perry used his few men shrewdly, making a show of being in fighting form. Perry shouted below for the surgeon's mates, the chaplain—even the wounded were put back in the fight. Still, it wasn't enough. One officer came begging for new gunners fully five times. Every gunner was hit as quickly as he could replace them. The fifth time Perry could only shake his head. There were no more men to put into action.

Finally, a British cannonball battered the *Lawrence's* last working gun into silence.

Perry's younger brother, barely in his teens, raced through the wreckage. Gunfire had ripped his hat and coat. "Let me at a gun!" he cried, "Let me at them!" But there were no more guns.

Eighteen crew members were still on their feet, ready to fight on—but with what? Perry was desperate. Where was the *Niagara*? What was wrong with Elliott? Perry made a quick decision. If Elliott wouldn't bring the *Niagara* to battle, then Perry would. "Lower a rowboat," he roared. "I'll fetch her!"

His men watched him go. "If victory is to be gained today," he called to them, "I'll gain it!" One of them thought the *Lawrence* was sinking and that Perry was running away. The angry sailor threw after him the blue flag bearing Lawrence's last words. Perry caught it, hoisted it and pointed to it defiantly. It was a gesture the men understood, and they all cheered.

The boatmen pulled on the oars, making their way toward the *Niagara*. Musket balls and shells flew about them. Perry stood erect in the boat, straining to see the enemy's ships. "What's wrong?" Perry demanded when the men stopped rowing.

"Sit down!" they yelled, "or you'll get us all killed." Perry sat, and the rowing resumed. He soon was aboard the *Niagara*. There was no time to ask questions. He sent Elliott down into the rowboat with orders to go to one of the smaller American ships and bring it into the action.

Then he shouted his orders. "Full sail! We're going toward the enemy—not away from her!" He signaled his other ships: "Close Action!"

Seeing what was happening now, the captain of the British ship *Queen Charlotte* tried to turn to aid the *Detroit*. It was a mistake. The *Queen Charlotte* ran her bowsprit into the *Detroit's* rigging. Now the two British ships were tangled together, unable to move.

It was a stroke of luck and Perry seized it. He ordered the full force of the *Niagara's* deadly firepower on the *Detroit* and *Queen Charlotte.* After just seven minutes the British ships struck their colors. They lowered Great Britain's proud flag as a sign of surrender. Two other British ships soon gave up as well. The last two tried to flee to the safety of the Canadian shore. The American *Scorpion* and *Trippe* went after them and caught them.

The battle was over. With the captured ships Perry found himself in charge of nearly twice as many ships as he had that morning. To this day the Battle of Lake Erie is the only battle in which an entire British fleet was lost.

Perry had to get the news to General Harrison, quickly. With Lake Erie under American control, Harrison's army could be carried to Canada to fight the British there.

Hastily, Perry took pen in hand.

"We have met the enemy," he wrote to Harrison, "and they are ours."

To learn more...

The exciting story of Perry's victory and many others is told in *The Age of Fighting Sail: The Story of the Naval War of 1812* by C. S. Forester. Also worthwhile is Richard Dillon's biography, *We Have Met the Enemy: Oliver Hazard Perry, Wilderness Commander* (New York: McGraw-Hill, 1978).

The Perry's Victory and International Peace Memorial is on South Bass Island. From its tower you can look over the lake where the battle was fought. Exhibits about the War of 1812 are in the Lake Erie Islands Historical Society Museum at 441 Catawba Ave., Put-in-Bay. Telephone (419) 285-2804.

Perry's brig *Niagara* has been restored to sailing condition and can be seen at home port in Erie, Pennsylvania; tel. (814) 452-2744. Its story can be found on the World Wide Web at <http://www.ncinter.net/~niagara>.

Rescuer of Slaves:

John Parker
1827-1900

Are you famous? Neither was John Parker. His work was secret and few have heard of him. But even if hardly anybody knows what you've done, you can still be a hero.

John Parker
lived in this house (center picture),
which still stands in Ripley. He helped
slaves escape across the Ohio River (top)
and begin their journey north
to freedom (bottom).

You could tell John Parker was free by the way he walked: chin up, shoulders back. No matter that there was a price on the black man's head. His strides were long and purposeful.

This dark night he strode to the edge of Ripley, Ohio, then slipped into the little wilderness of weeds along the shore of the broad Ohio River. He was on a dangerous mission from which he might not return. He thought of his wife Miranda and their seven children back in Ripley. He wondered again how they would manage if he should be caught and killed. But then he thought of another family, a Kentucky slave couple and their baby. They longed to be free and he had to risk helping them.

He knew what it was to be a slave; he had been one himself. Now a free man, he owned an Ohio foundry. He'd come a long way.

Parker found a rowboat he'd hidden and was soon afloat. Ripley shrank to a few distant lights on the north shore. One of those lights was from his own home. Another was from the home of the Rev. John Rankin, his wife Jean and their children. No finer folks than those. He could see that light now, shining from the front window of the Rankin house high on the bluff.

The light from the Rankin house was a signal light for escaped slaves crossing the Ohio River. If they could find their way to that house, they'd be given food and shelter. They would also get a safe ride to the next station on what was called the Underground Railroad. This was a secret network of people who helped slaves escape. Many of those people lived in Ohio.

There was a price on the Reverend Rankin's head, too. Kentucky slave owners had offered $2,500 to anyone who would kill John Rankin. The Reverend Rankin was not just a minister. He was an abolitionist—someone who wanted to abolish slavery. He was also one of the most active "conductors" on the Underground Railroad.

John Parker smiled grimly when he thought of how much his own dead body would bring. Slipping in and out of Kentucky on his slave rescue missions, he had sometimes seen a "Wanted "poster:

Reward of $1000 for John Parker,
Dead or Alive

Parker looked over his shoulder at the pitch-dark south shore. Danger lay that way, but that was where he was headed–to Kentucky, a slave state. Strange that a free-flowing river could mark the border between a land where slavery was legal and a land where it was not. It was against the law to own a slave in Ohio. However, it was also against the law to aid a runaway slave.

Parker respected the law of the land, but he had a higher respect for God's law. He believed that God meant humans to be free.

He was drawing near Kentucky now. He knew that shore well; dozens of times he'd come on such missions. He hid the boat and was soon afoot on the River Road. He passed a farmhouse, lamps twinkling behind leaf-screened windows.

Finally John Parker came to the crossroads at the corner of the Shrofes' farm. He slipped into the cornfield and silently made his way down the rows. At the window of a slave cabin he'd secretly visited before, he whispered low.

There was a muffled reply, a shuffling and rustling. Then a young man came out. "We can't go," he whispered in Parker's ear.

"What? Why not? Don't you want to be free?"

"Yes, sir, more than anything, but we can't go because...." The young man made a strange noise and Parker thought he was choking. Then he realized the sounds were sobs. From behind him, his wife said in a soft, firm voice, "We won't go without our baby."

"Mister Shrofe keeps the baby in his bedroom at night," the husband explained. "He has a loaded pistol and a lit candle on the table alongside. He knows we're never going to leave without our baby."

Parker thought of his own baby, sleeping at home. His mouth went dry and his stomach welled up. He curled his huge, iron-worker's hands into fists. He thought how much easier it would be simply to kill his people's enemies. But no, he would not do that.

"Wait here," he told the couple. "When I come back with the child, you be ready to run like you never ran before."

Soon Parker was at Shrofe's kitchen door. Then he was inside, feeling his way through the darkness to the front stair.

Half-way up, Parker froze. He heard something. A faint, regular sound, like the low moan of bellows. In the darkness, Parker's lips bent into a thin smile. It was the sound of snoring, coming from behind a closed door at the top of the stairs.

He dropped to his hands and knees and slowly pushed the door open. The faint grinding of the hinges barely reached his ear, but in the dark it seemed like the mighty surge of a huge machine. Inch by inch, the door swung to, until the opening was wide enough for him to crawl through. He moved like a box turtle, as slow as the seasons. Barely two feet from him lay old Shrofe, eyes closed, snoring softly.

Parker rounded the foot of the bed and there was the baby, sound asleep on a pillow, lashes lowered over fat cheeks. Then he saw the pistol, on the table, next to the candle.

Parker picked up the baby, pillow and all, and rose to his knees. Shrofe rolled over and opened his eyes half-way, then closed them again and sighed deeply. Parker rose to his full height and took a step toward the door, babe in arms. Shrofe blinked twice and turned his head. He was staring dully up at the big, black man. For a moment, Parker thought the old man would close his eyes again and go back to sleep. Instead he jerked his head and sat up.

Parker threw the pillow at the candle, snuffing it and sweeping the pistol off the table. Even before it hit the floor, Parker was out the door and half-way down the stairs. Shrofe was yelling as he bumped in the dark, scrambling for a light and his pistol.

Out the kitchen door, across the yard sped Parker, his legs pumping. He reached the couple's cabin. Without a word they fell in behind him, the three of them racing across the cornfield toward the crossroad. Shrofe was shouting and firing pistol shots into the air, but the sounds were quickly growing faint behind them.

They ran along the dusty road for half a mile, silent except for their terrible gasping. The woman began to slow. "Go on!" She heaved the words out. "Go on without me!" Her husband slowed too, grabbed her wrist and then ran again as hard as he could, pulling her behind him, her legs whirling like a mill wheel.

Another quarter mile and they turned, crashing through the weeds to the river's edge. Parker thrust the baby into the mother's arms and the couple scrambled into the boat. Parker shoved the boat into the current, springing to his seat at the last second.

Parker made the oars fly like the wings of a bird while the father paddled the water with arms grown strong from hard labor. The boat thrust ahead and the Kentucky shore faded into the darkness.

Then they heard shouts coming from the Kentucky side. Shrofe was still after them.

"Get down," Parker cried out. The mother slid to the bottom of the boat, curling herself round the baby. The father paddled even harder, splashing cold water onto Parker's head and shoulders.

Pulling the oars with all his might, Parker watched the dark shore. Tiny points of reddish-yellow light caught his eye. A second later the crack-crack of rifle shots rang out. More followed and Parker heard bullets whizzing past them in the dark.

He rowed as hard as he could, his chest heaving, his back and arms and legs moving steadily as he put an ever greater distance between himself and his enemies, between his human cargo and their pursuers, between slave state and free.

Finally they reached the Ohio shore and safety. The gunshots had stopped; Shrofe had given up.

Parker took the rescued family to the Rankin house. From there, in the nights that followed, they were whisked on to Canada where they would be free.

So it was with hundreds, even thousands, of escaping slaves. The road to freedom was a north-bound road. The Underground Railroad, they called it. But none could make the journey without the concern, the help, and the raw courage of people like John Parker and the Rev. Rankin, his wife Jean, their children, and many others.

To learn more...

John Parker was one of the few former slaves who is able to speak to us today. He tells his story in his own words in *His Promised Land: The Autobiography of John P. Parker, Former Slave and Conductor on the Underground Railroad*, edited by Stuart Seely Sprague (New York: W.W. Norton, 1996). The book is highly recommended.

The Underground Railroad station run in Ripley by the Rev. John Rankin is now a museum of the Ohio Historical Society. Telephone (937) 392-1627.

Black resistance to slavery is illustrated on a fascinating World Wide Web site: <http://afroam.org/history/slavery/index.html>. The Library of Congress offers excellent resources, including "The African-American Mosaic" at http://lcweb.loc.gov/exhibits/african/intro.html>.

6

One Cause of the Big War:

Harriet Beecher Stowe
1811-1896

Hatty Stowe's Cincinnati years were hard. Very hard. But she used the memory of her misery to write one of the few books that really did change the world.

Harriet Beecher Stowe
gathered ideas for her blockbuster book,
Uncle Tom's Cabin, while living in Cincinnati.
Today, her home there is a museum.

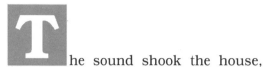he sound shook the house, wrenching Hatty from deep sleep.

She swung her feet to the cool floor–the house was stifling hot–and went to the window. Dear God, let it be only thunder, she prayed. She peered to the west. No, the stars shone brightly.

It was trouble downtown, she knew. She pushed the front door open and stepped outside. She peered toward the riverfront, the heart of Cincinnati. Rising columns of smoke could be dimly seen.

The sound came again–a short, blunt bark that shook the air. Were they blowing things up? There was a rustle behind her. Her five-year-old twins, Eliza and little Harriet, had also been awakened. She felt the soft, warm grip of their hands taking hers.

The three stood in silence, listening. There was another sound, too– the muffled, crackling sound of gunfire, like popcorn popping far away. There were faint screams and shouts as well.

A third time the huge rumbling sound reached them. Hatty's boarders came out now. "It's the riots," one of them said. "But where did they get a cannon?"

"A cannon?" gasped Hatty. The twins moved closer.

"It surely is. I often heard that sound during the war."

Hatty looked up again at the stars. God's creation was lovely, she thought, but people were sometimes so wicked.

Three months earlier a man named Burnett hid a runaway slave. The Kentucky owner of the slave came to Burnett's door and a fight broke out. Burnett was put in jail, which made many people angry. The city was tense during the summer. There was a murder and other violence. Then, just as people were hoping September would bring a cooling of tempers, a street fight turned into a race riot.

Blacks and whites ran through the streets, firing guns, hurling rocks, clubbing one another. A cannon was found and the streets of the African-American part of town were raked and rocked by its blasts.

Finally the state militia forced an uneasy peace on Cincinnati. Frightened young mothers like Hatty Stowe could again go to market, basket in hand.

The riots were only the latest thing to trouble Harriet Beecher Stowe, whom everyone called Hatty. Her life had not gone as expected. She had wanted to be a writer, but marriage and motherhood tied her down. She loved her children dearly, but felt no more free than a slave. Her father, a famous preacher, bossed the family. Her husband, Calvin, was a bumbler who often thought he was sick. He would take to his bed, raving hopelessly. Hatty would have to bring him hot soup.

Hatty's life grew harder each year. Even as it did, she would sometimes feel herself gripped by a story she had heard in her girlhood.

Hatty had gone with her father to Ripley, Ohio, a town fifty miles upriver from Cincinnati. They stayed in the home of the Rev. John Rankin, where they had noticed something strange. A lamp was left burning, all night long, in the window facing the river. Hatty asked why.

Reverend Rankin said in a low voice that the lamp was a signal for runaway slaves on the Kentucky side of the river. If they could reach his home, they would get food and shelter. Then someone would take them to the next safe stop north on the Underground Railroad.

Reverend Rankin told stories about the many slaves he had helped since he first lit his lamp in 1825. She remembered one story most of all.

It had happened in March, several years before. A spell of warm weather was cracking the ice that covered the wide Ohio River. An escaped slave woman, her baby in her arms, stood on the Kentucky shore. She could see the warm glow of the Rankins' light. The ice stretched away before her, dappled with dark puddles and cracks. She took a deep breath and darted onto the ice.

After a few yards, her bare feet slipped and she fell. She leaped up again and kept running. Again and again she fell and got up, until she was soaking wet, her teeth chattering with the cold. Finally she reached the Ohio shore. Then she made the long, hard climb to the Rankins' house.

The Rankins gave the woman dry clothes and warm food. After a short rest, the Reverend drove her north in his wagon. On his return he heard a terrible roar coming up the valley. The ice on the river was breaking into huge chunks that crashed against each other. The woman and her baby had crossed the river just in time.

That slave woman was free now, but Hatty felt as if there were no escape for her. Her duties at home bound her like chains. Still more children came, six in all, leaving Hatty poorer than ever. It seemed as if things could hardly get worse. But they did.

A disease called cholera was a grim summer visitor to hot, humid Cincinnati in those days. People knew nothing about germs and drank unclean water. The summer of 1849 was the worst. Hundreds died, then thousands. In a single day 120 funerals passed the Stowe house.

One day the Stowe's little dog Daisy suddenly had fits and died a half hour later. Then more bad news came. The old black woman who had done their washing only the day before had died of cholera that morning, too.

Two days later, Hatty's baby died. Hatty's husband and father were out of town. With only her other children to comfort her, Hatty buried her baby. Then she wrote to her husband, Calvin: "In this city [there is] scarce a house without its dead. This heartbreak, this anguish, has been everywhere, and when it will end God alone knows."

Finally, the epidemic ended. It had killed 4,500 people. .

Then Calvin came home with some good news for a change. He had a new job as a teacher in Maine. Hatty and the children left at once for Maine. They wanted to avoid another cholera season and to protect the new life–her seventh child–that was growing within her.

Something else was growing within her as well. It was an idea for a book. A grand idea, sweeping and passionate. Hatty started to write. Somehow she found the time. Instead of just wishing she could be a writer, she became one.

As she wrote, she thought of the stories she had heard back in Ohio. Most of all, she remembered the runaway slave woman crossing the river with her baby just before the ice broke.

Hatty remembered other stories. Her brother Charles had gone south to work in New Orleans. He was soon back in Cincinnati, full of terrible tales of slavery. He told Hatty about a cruel Yankee slave boss on a farm in Louisiana. The slave master told Charles to feel his fist, bragging that it "had got as hard as iron by knocking down niggers."

With stories like these in mind, Harriet Beecher Stowe wrote *Uncle Tom's Cabin*. The book came out in 1852 and stunned the nation. It went on to become one of the most famous books of all time. It was all made-up, a work of fiction, but it was based on facts.

Millions of readers of *Uncle Tom's Cabin* found their hearts pounding as they read about the escaped slave Eliza. They read how Eliza clasped her baby and crossed the Ohio River by jumping from one floating ice cake to another.

A young girl named Eva was another person in Hatty's book. People around the world were touched by the illness and death of the innocent little Eva. And they would flinch in horror at the story of the evil, drunken slave master, named Simon Legree. Legree killed the kindly old slave Uncle Tom, lashing him to death.

Hatty put into her book all the fury, tenderness and passion that had filled her life during her 18 years in Cincinnati. But the book did more than thrill her readers. It also made them see just how terrible slavery was. Many people had opposed slavery before the book. But *Uncle Tom's Cabin* made the horrors of slavery come alive for them. It made them willing to fight to end it.

Soon American was at war with itself. The Civil War began in 1861, less than 10 years after Hatty Stowe's book was published.

Now Hatty was the most famous author in America. She even met President Abraham Lincoln. He shook her hand and said, "So this is the little woman who wrote the book that caused the big war."

Like Hatty, Abe Lincoln had a way with words. And he had it right. Using only the power of words, a little woman named Hatty Stowe helped to change history.

To learn more...

Young readers will enjoy *Harriet Beecher Stowe and the Beecher Preachers*, by Jean Fritz (New York: Putnam, 1994). Another enjoyable book for young readers is *Harriet: the Life and World of Harriet Beecher Stowe,* by Norma Johnston (Peach Tree Books, 1996). The author's life is treated in greater detail in Suzanne M. Coil's *Harriet Beecher Stowe* (New York: Franklin Watts, 1993).

At the Harriet Beecher Stowe House, 2950 Gilbert Ave., Cincinnati, you can see exhibits about the abolitionist movement, the history of African-Americans, and the Beecher family. Telephone (513) 632-5120. The Rankin house in nearby Ripley is also a museum (see "To learn more" following the chapter on John Parker).

World Wide Web sites of interest include *Chris's Home Page* at <http://www.ucc.uconn.edu:80/~cep95002/>.

7

The Great Locomotive Chase:

Jacob Parrott
1843-1908

Heroes don't always work alone, nor always succeed. Take this story of a famous chase. The heroes work together, risk all and fail. Yet, their courage makes them heroes.

Andrews' Raiders,
all Ohioans, included Jacob Parrott
the youngest member. The Raid,
in which a Rebel train was stolen (top),
earned Parrott the nation's first
Congressional Medal of Honor.

One April morning in 1862, twenty strange men got on a train in Marietta, Georgia. Marietta was deep in the heart of the Confederate states of the South, which were at war with the Union states of the North. Someone should have asked those strangers who they were. But the Civil War seemed far away to people in Marietta. No one suspected a thing.

The men were spies. They had strolled up, one by one, to the station's ticket window. They had coolly bought their tickets with Confederate dollars. Pretending not to know each other, they quietly took their seats on the train.

In those days, railroads often gave names to their best engines. This train was one of the Western & Atlantic Railroad's best. The engine was named the General.

The leader of the strangers was a tall, thin man with a long dark beard. His name was James J. Andrews. Andrews was not a Union soldier. Instead, he was a daring, bold, full-time spy for the Union.

The rest of his men were Yankee soldiers from Ohio. They were young; one, Jacob Parrott, was barely 18. The men had offered to go on a raid behind enemy lines, knowing nothing about it except that it would be risky.

When the train reached Big Shanty, the other riders got off for breakfast. Then Andrews' men swung into action. They unhitched a few cars of the train to block the track. Then they leapt aboard the remaining section. Their goal was astounding: They were going to steal a train out from under the noses of the Rebels!

A Rebel sentry watched the strangers but asked no questions. Andrews and three men climbed into the cab of the General. The rest got in the last car. But the men forgot to cut the train's bell cord.

As the stolen train began to move, a loud clang of its alarm bell brought its crew running. The Rebel crew followed on foot at first, then by handcar. The chase began much sooner than Andrews had expected.

Even so, all went well for the raiders at first. The stolen train slowly picked up speed. Andrews planned to go at the train's usual speed at first. He would speed up later.

A few miles north, the raiders stopped briefly. Some of the men cut telegraph wires. Others loaded crossties onto the stolen train. They planned to use them later to burn bridges behind them.

The stolen train soon stopped again, this time to take on fuel and water. Andrews was able to fool the Rebel station master into thinking everything was all right. But the station master warned Andrews that recent rainstorms were making all the trains run late. Andrews could not travel as fast he had planned.

Two hours soon passed as they glided past towns and stations far behind enemy lines. Come this time tomorrow, the raiders thought, we'll be back in camp, telling our story.

Then came Kingston. The stolen train had to wait on a sidetrack while a Rebel freight train rumbled slowly southward. When it was finally gone, Andrews' sigh of relief was cut short. One of the raiders pointed out a red flag waving from the other train's last car. It meant that a second train was close behind!

More and more time was being lost. The raiders could only wait in agony. But this train also displayed a red flag. Still another train was coming! The tension was almost more than they could bear.

Local trainmen saw the General and began to ask questions. Andrews lied to them, but also quietly told his men: "Be ready to fight." However, the skillful Andrews fooled the Southerners once again.

Finally the third freight train passed and the General chugged northward. Sixty-five minutes had been lost. None of the raiders knew it yet, but their chance of success had also been lost.

Meanwhile, the Southerners were in hot pursuit in another engine. They got to Kingston, ready to fight. There they were stalled by the same freight trains that had stopped the General. But they were lucky: there was still another engine, the Rome mail train, steamed up and ready to roll, on a sidetrack just a half mile away. So the Rebels bypassed the traffic jam, unhitched the Rome train's engine, and charged on. Now there was nothing but open track ahead!

The raiders stopped to tear up the tracks behind them. They could not have guessed that the Rebels were so close behind. Suddenly, they heard the noise of another train. It was the Rebel engine, bearing down on them with a great cloud of smoke. The Yankees tumbled back on board their own train and fled northward.

A frantic hour followed. Armed only with pistols, the raiders dared not risk an open fight. At last, however, they stopped long enough to jam the track behind them with a crosstie.

The General flew past Adairsville where another engine, the Texas, happened to be waiting on a sideline. Andrews was frantic to reach the sideline at Calhoun Station before the express train came through. Nine miles flew by in as many minutes, the whistle screaming. Suddenly the express train came into view. A head-on crash seemed certain. But no! The other train had heard their whistle and was backing up to allow the General to reach the sideline.

But Fuller and his men were close behind. Now they ran on foot to Adairsville and took over the Texas. The Southerners came on them just as they were starting to tear up tracks, forcing them to flee.

Near Resaca the raiders stopped to unhitch their boxcars. They hoped their pursuers would crash into them. But the Rebels just slowed down and nudged the cars to a sideline.

Next, the raiders tried to set a long covered bridge on fire, but rain doused the flames. On they went. They rounded curves at breakneck speed, hoping not to jump the track. The General clung to the rails, but every time it reached a straightaway, there was the Texas, coming up from behind.

The raiders tried their crosstie trick again. They jammed the rails on a curve that Fuller couldn't see until he was almost on it. The Texas rammed the crosstie and bucked like a bronco. Somehow the crosstie was pushed aside and the engine roared on past.

Andrews had another idea. He ordered the walls of their last boxcar to be pulled down, piled on the floor, and set afire. With the wind whipping up the fire, the boxcar was soon in flames. Then it was unhitched and left inside a covered bridge. All twenty raiders crowded into the cab of the General, and the weary soldiers rolled on.

But the Southerners in the Texas hardly paused. They rolled through the thick smoke inside the covered bridge. They pushed the burning car to the far side of the river and tipped it over, then resumed the chase.

After ninety miles, the General's fuel was gone and it slowed to a halt. The raiders scattered into the woods. In the next few days all of them were captured and jailed. The Rebels' quick response, together with the rain, had undone the brave Yankee raid.

Seven raiders, including Andrews, were hung as spies. Others, including Parrott were put in prison. Parrott was whipped by his captors but bravely refused to reveal secrets of the raiders. Some escaped but were caught again and clapped into irons. A few others fled north, and a few stole all the way to Florida where they were picked up by a Northern gunboat.

Andrews' Raiders had failed. They had been unable to steal a Rebel train after all. They had not even been able to wreck any track or burn a single bridge. Yet something was gained after all. The story of the daring raid fired the pride of the Northern people. It renewed their ability to fight on and to win.

Finally, in March of 1863, all the members of Andrews' Raiders who were left came to Washington. Secretary of War William Stanton was also an Ohioan. He praised the men for their bravery and told them that their state and their nation were proud of their service.

Then he gave each of the Ohioans a glittering badge. It was a new kind of award, Stanton said. It was to be given only to those American soldiers who had shown the most outstanding courage. It had been created for the survivors of what came to be known as the Great Locomotive Chase. It was to be called the Congressional Medal of Honor.

To this day the Medal of Honor is still America's highest award for bravery. The very first to win it were the Ohioans known as Andrews' Raiders. And, because of his youth and bravery under torture, Parrott was the first of the Ohioans to be given the medal.

To learn more...

One of the raiders was William Pittenger. Starting in 1863, and for many years, he told the story of the raid over and over again, in books with titles such as *Capturing a Locomotive* and *The Great Locomotive Chase.* Most Ohio libraries have at least one of Pittenger's books.

Hollywood's version of the story, also called *The Great Locomotive Chase,* appeared in 1956. A 1927 movie classic, *The General,* starred Buster Keaton in a hilarious, inventive and not very accurate version of events. Both films are available on video.

At least 10 veterans of the Andrews Raid rest in cemeteries in Ohio. Jacob Parrott, the first American to get the Congressional Medal of Honor, was buried in Grove Cemetery, Kenton. Other Ohio burial sites include the Bowling Green area, Coulton, Columbus, Dowling, McComb, the Pemberville area, Stryker and Toledo.

"The General," fully restored, is on display in the Kennesaw Civil War Museum in Georgia. More information on "The Great Locomotive Chase" can be seen on the museum's web site: <http://www.ngeorgia.com/history/kcwm.shtml>.

8

Mother of the Battlefield:

Mary Ann Bickerdyke

1817-1901

Not all heroes are handsome or pretty. This lady wasn't pretty. Neither was the work she did. But it was important work and she had the guts to do it.

Mary Ann Bickerdyke
rushed to comfort sick and wounded
Union soldiers in the Civil War.
Sometimes even barns were used
as hospitals (top). Today her statue
stands in Galesburg, Illinois.

Big-boned, plain-faced, wide-bottomed Mary Ann Bickerdyke slapped the reins. The horses pulled just a little harder. Poor babies, she thought. They'd already come a long way. She wished she could give them a rest. But her wagon load of supplies was badly needed by the wounded Yankee soldiers at the hospital tent camp in Cairo, Illinois. Hearing about them at church, Mary Ann had gathered what was needed and set out.

It wasn't the first time she'd traveled alone. She'd hauled runaway slaves, hidden in her wagon, from Cincinnati to Dayton. As a healer who knew all about steam baths and medicine plants, Mary Ann had often gone alone to visit the sick. A widow with two sons to raise had to learn to do for herself.

Tough as she was, she was shocked by what she saw in the Army hospital tents. But she didn't shy away. She got busy.

She put the stronger patients to work. With their help, she bedded the wounded on fresh straw. She sawed barrels in two for bathtubs. She cut the men's hair short so that the bugs nesting there could be killed.

She wrote to her church, asking for fresh pillowcases, flannel blankets, men's underwear, and soap, soap, soap—plenty of soap! She called for skillets, pots and pans, kettles and washtubs. She said she wasn't going home until "these poor, wounded boys" got the care they so badly needed.

Before she got to Cairo, the wounded had cooked for themselves. The bad food made them even sicker. Now Mary Ann took over the cooking. In her plain Quaker clothes and stiff straw bonnet, she soon earned the nickname of "Mother Bickerdyke."

She had more to fight than wounds and sickness. Other people's bad ideas got in her way. Women were not supposed to go into hospital tents. She talked her way past the guards anyway. She said "the boys" were more important than army rules.

Everyone thought the war would end quickly, so nobody bothered much with hospitals. But Mother Bickerdyke knew how stubborn Americans could be. She settled in for a long haul.

But a volunteer could only get so far past Army rules. Although she lived in Galesburg, Illinois, Mary Ann Bickerdyke had been born in Knox County, Ohio. She had also lived in Richland, Lorain and Hamilton counties. General Grant was another Ohioan, and she knew he'd see sense. She got him to sign a note making her the "matron" of the first military hospital for the western battlefields. Nobody knew how much bossing a "matron" could do, but Mother Bickerdyke made the most of it.

She found that hospital supplies were being stolen by healthy soldiers, so she complained to the head doctor. He sniffed and told her that women had no business around the army. She was a troublemaker, he said. She could pack her bags and go home.

"Doctor," she said, staring into his eyes, "I'm here to stay as long as the men need me. If you put me out of one door, I'll come in at another. If you bar all the doors against me, I'll come in at the window. If anybody goes from here, it'll be YOU. I'm going straight to General Grant!"

This was not what the doctor expected. He knew she meant every word. He said that he'd make sure there was no more stealing.

But nothing changed. One day Mary Ann spotted a young officer hanging around the hospital. The wounded soldiers' lunches couldn't be served because he was talking with the cooks. His army jacket was open, and Mother Bickerdyke grew very interested in–his undershirt! She sneaked up behind him. Then she jerked off his coat and pulled back the undershirt collar. There, plain to see, were the letters "NWSC," meaning Northwestern Sanitary Commission. That shirt was stolen! Big Mother Bickerdyke furiously threw the amazed young man to the floor. Then, she SAT on him–and yanked off his shirt. With a yell, she held it high for the cheering wounded soldiers to see.

When he got to his feet, she stood before him, hands on her hips. "You ain't sick," she said. "NWSC stuff is for sick men, not you Now get on with your work. These boys have waited too long already."

Mother Bickerdyke was even rougher on food thieves. She knew that some officers and cooks stole and ate the best food. But she was told she couldn't prove it. She thought over the matter and set up a little trap.

One day a case of beautiful dried peaches arrived in the hospital kitchen. Mary Ann lit a stove and began stewing the peaches in butter, brown sugar and cinnamon. Soon the delicious smell began to spread round the hospital. She poured the fruit into pie plates and set them on a window sill to cool.

"These is for the boys," she told the cook. "They'll cool in time for supper and I'll be back to give 'em out myself. They ain't enough to go round, so I aim to see they get to the boys what needs 'em most. Don't you touch 'em. And see that nobody else touches 'em neither. This is patients' food."

The cook glared at her. No one on his staff EVER touched patients' food, he growled.

Mary Ann left without a word and went back to caring for "the boys." From the corner of her eye she saw that a lot of healthy soldiers were dropping by the kitchen. Was it because of those peach pies? She gave the wounded a wink and whispered, "Just you wait and see what happens."

Strange sounds soon began to come from the kitchen. A hubbub of choking, gagging and spewing noises became so loud that the patients rose to their elbows. Mother Bickerdyke went to check it out. In the kitchen she found a dozen men on the floor, wiggling in pain, grabbing their bellies and throwing up.

"What's the matter, fellows?" she asked. "Peaches don't agree with you?" No one answered. "Well, let me tell you, you're lucky. Hush up now, you ain't going to die. Not this time. All you got was a little tartar to clean you out. But hear me out! Next time, it's going to be rat poison I put in the food you steal and then you WILL have something to cry about!"

But not even this trick stopped the stealing. So Mother Bickerdyke finally reported to the highest generals. The cook and his men were jailed and then moved to the front lines, far away from hospital kitchens.

Mary Ann Bickerdyke became a hero to the Yankee Army. She was as famous for standing up to officers and doctors as for the comfort she gave the wounded. Reporters wrote newspaper stories about her work. They told how she searched for wounded soldiers in the dark on the night after a battle. Sometimes she faced terrible things. Once she had to use a hatchet to chop the wounded free from where they lay. Left behind in the winter cold, they had frozen to the ground in puddles of their own blood.

When she took over the care of the wounded after the battle of Shiloh, an army doctor tried to stop her. Where did she get her authority, he demanded. "I have received my authority from the Lord God Almighty," she snapped. "Have you anything that ranks higher than that?"

She was made an agent of the Sanitary Commission, visiting hospital camps on a bony horse she named "Old Whitey." She learned she could raise money for her work by giving speeches about her healing tricks and adventures But she never stayed away for long from "the boys" who needed her.

Mother Bickerdyke marched with Ohio's General William Tecumseh Sherman as his armies fought their way south. When food ran low, she went back north, rounded up cows and chickens and led the beasts in a moo-ing, cackling parade back to the Yankee camp.

Her legend grew. Some said she baked 100 pies in a single day, or was it 500 loaves of bread? She washed a thousand undershirts, or was it two thousand blankets? The soldiers loved her, the doctors and cooks were afraid of her, and the generals respected her. Her friend General Sherman called her "Mrs. Bickerdyke." She called him "Bill." When someone asked General Sherman why he let her break army rules, he simply said, "She outranks me."

In April of 1865 the war was finally won. Mother Bickerdyke proudly took her place among the soldiers in the great victory parade. Stately and grave in her in Quaker clothes and bonnet, she rode "Old Whitey" through the streets of Washington, D.C.

No one deserved that moment of glory more than Mary Ann Bickerdyke...an angel of mercy born and raised in Ohio.

To learn more...

The thrilling life story of Mary Ann Bickerdyke is told in a book titled *Cyclone in Calico*, by Nina Brown Baker (Boston: Little, Brown, 1952). Although she was born in Ohio and often travelled there, the state has no relics of Mother Bickerdyke's life and service. However, in a public square in Galesburg, Illinois, there is a handsome monument, erected in 1904. It shows the heroic nurse kneeling beside a wounded soldier and holding a cup to his lips. Mother Bickerdyke lies buried in Linwood Cemetery, Galesburg. "The Role of women in the Civil War" is an interesting web site at <http://www.glue.umd.edu/~cliswp/history/cwar>.

9

Grant's Last Battle:

Ulysses S. Grant
1822-1885

*Grant saved the Union by winning Civil War battles.
His last battle was different. He took on an enemy he
could not beat. This time he fought to save his family.*

Ulysses S. Grant
looked like this when he
was a young soldier (bottom)
and like this (center) as leader
of the Union army in the Civil War.
The top picture shows him
only days before his death.

e wasn't clever, and he wasn't easy on the eyes. As a boy, Ulysses S. Grant looked as rumpled at noon as he did when he first wriggled out of bed. His neighbors in Georgetown, Ohio, liked him all right. But no one expected him to amount to much.

He was amazingly good with horses, an important skill in those days. But that alone would not take him far. He went to West Point, but even the spit-and-polish of that tough military school did not change him. The young soldier met Colonel Robert E. Lee during the Mexican War. The older officer had to remind Grant that "an officer reporting at headquarters should be in full uniform."

They met again eighteen years later, when General Lee surrendered. Nothing had changed. Lee was trim, brilliant and proud. Grant was rumpled.

In the years between those two meetings, even Grant's life had become badly rumpled. When the Mexican War was over, he got plopped in a dusty California army fort, far from his wife and kids. Boredom and whiskey were always there in large amounts. Grant soon became known as a drunk, a bad rap he never quite shook. Later, out of the Army and back east with his family again, he quit drinking.

Then he set about failing at one thing after another. First he failed as a farmer, then as a rent collector, finally as a shop clerk. He was too poor even to own a horse. He was a nobody, a complete flop.

And yet....

There was something to the fellow after all. Something fearsome and flinty. His scruffy beard hid a strong jaw. His eyes were cold as steel. When the time came, he faced his weakness for strong drink, clamped his jaws shut and licked it. Horseless, staring his way to work and home again, he shrugged off the notion that he was a nobody, shrugged it off like rain.

Then the Civil War came, and Grant went back to being a soldier. He shrugged off the fancy uniforms and the fancy notions of other generals. He settled down to fight, doing nothing fancy, just slugging away. And winning battles. Small ones at first, then bigger ones. Pretty soon President Lincoln noticed him. Lincoln decided this was the man he wanted to lead his entire army.

As the Civil War dragged on, some leaders found it hard to stay on task. But with that hard stare of his, Grant could see something they didn't. In battle, he stared and struck, stared and struck. He was blind, some said, to the cost in lost lives. But he kept winning. He stared down General Johnston in the West and he stared down General Lee in the East. Both surrendered.

When the war was over, America swept Grant into the White House. But he found being President harder than quitting drink or winning battles. Surrounded by cheaters and thieves, he stared through two terms, doing almost nothing, waiting and all but silent.

Travel came next. For almost three years he checked countries off the list. He was looking all over the world for something to do. Home at last in New York City, he loaned his good name and all his money to a certain Ferdinand Ward. Grant & Ward, their company was called. Grant was the most famous man in America and many people trusted him to take care of their money.

Ward stole it. All of it. Grant's money and everybody else's. Everybody else who had trusted him.

Grant came home, a beaten man. His wife saw it at once. There was a crack in the stare.

Between them, the Grants had only $240.

There was nothing else.

And yet there was. In 1884 Grant wrote a story for a magazine about one of his Civil War battles. The story was a success. Now he stared into his own past and set about earning money for his family by using a pen. General Grant's pen wrote down General Grant's memories of General Grant's thoughts and feelings. No one else could write such things. He was a commander again—this time, a commander of words. He found he had a gift for commanding armies of words.

More stories followed. Clearly, the next thing to do was write a book.

Then, just as he was starting, another enemy struck Grant.

It was cancer of the throat—a rebel army of tiny cancer cells rising up against his body. From the start, Grant knew that this was a battle he would lose.

All right. Let Death take him, Grant thought. What difference would it make? He was sixty-three years old. He had no gripes. Who before him had ever seen and done the things he'd done? He'd go quietly...except for one thing. His family would be poor.

The book was his one hope. If he could hold off the Enemy, keep his head, steer clear of self-pity, force that pen across the page...maybe, just maybe he could finish the book, see it published, and earn some money for his family. Let him finish this book, please God, and then he'd surrender, unconditionally.

Grant's friend Mark Twain said he'd publish it. He called on Grant to make plans. He was shocked to see the general so thin and weak.

Reporters saw it, too. Soon everyone knew. Grant was dying.

By late March, 1885, he was coughing so hard that his face would go from the color of an onion to the color of a beet and then back again. Each attack left him weaker, yet he always rallied. Just as Lee had done.

Once, blood sopped his beard, shooting from his mouth and nose. The doctors raced to clear his throat. They stopped the bleeding just in time.

Grant worked on, gasping out the words for others to write down and then making changes in his own hand. His voice failed. It was an outpost fallen to the Enemy. He could no longer speak out the words he wanted in his book. But he kept writing.

Mid-June. New York City was terribly hot. Grant retreated north to a house in the cool, breezy Adirondack Mountains of upstate New York.

He spent hours sitting on the porch, wrapped in blankets. Writing, writing, he out-flanked Death with a pad and pencil, staring and striking. At last he was General Grant again, the old, cold-eyed Grant, out to finish the job.

Drugged for pain and sleep, he dozed. He seemed about to die but then amazed everyone by suddenly seeming strong again. Like Lee late in the war. Grant's sons read his writings to him; he signaled and scribbled, adding short thoughts, changing a word here and there.

He reinforced his strength as best he could, painfully swallowing beef broth mixed with eggs and milk.

When he let his head fall back, terrible coughs laid siege on him. From behind enemy lines, but close to the front, Death ordered the attacks. The choking coughs came like cavalry. The bursts of pain exploded like cannon shells, stabbed like bayonets. Supply lines grew thin, rations dwindled. Grant's failing strength fought hand-to-hand against the ever-oncoming tiredness. His lines were caving in. He knew the Enemy's plan. He saw that his final moment would come when, defenses gone, exhaustion had ground up his last reserves.

Grant struggled on, rewriting, rewriting. He could not stop working.

In early July, growing worse, he made his funeral plans. Then he rallied again, briefly but amazingly. His voice returned, and he ate with ease. He added a whole new opening section to his book.

The day came when the book finally seemed complete. The final draft was sent to Mark Twain.

Grant had outrun Death. Then it was the same as after both the Mexican War and the Civil War. The same as after his Presidency. Suddenly there was nothing left to do.

The last photo. Three days left to live. He is fully dressed, top hat and all. Legs crossed, at ease on his porch, reading a newspaper, he does not look like a man about to die.

He had seen the area's best view of the scenery only once, shortly after arriving. Now he wanted to see it again. His doctor didn't want him to make the little journey. When asked if he felt strong enough, the general nodded firmly. With sons and doctor pushing his wheelchair, he made the short ride to a mountain lookout. He could barely lift his eyes. He signaled to return. His strength was entirely gone.

The next morning, his last battle won, Grant surrendered. He died July 23, 1885.

To learn more...

The fascinating stories of both Grant and his Southern foe, Robert E. Lee, are well told for young readers in *A House Divided: The Lives of Ulysses S. Grant and Robert E. Lee*, by Jules Archer (New York: Scholastic, 1995). Also well written, but with much more detail, is Geoffrey Perret's *Ulysses S. Grant: Soldier and President* (New York: Random House, 1997), the latest of many biographies of Grant.

One of the best sites on the World Wide Web is "The Ulysses S. Grant Home Page" (http://www.mscomm.com/~ulysses/), rich with rare photographs, articles, a bibliography, and many useful links.

Grant's birthplace in Point Pleasant is now a museum of the Ohio Historical Society, open April through October. Phone 1-800-796-4282 or 1-800-BUCKEYE. His boyhood home in Georgetown and the schoolhouse he attended there are also run as museums by local volunteers. Call the Brown County Chamber of Commerce at (937) 378-4784 for information. Tours of the Georgetown sites led by a man dressed as Grant are possible by special arrangement.

A Thousand Inventions:

Thomas Alva Edison
1847-1931

Thomas Edison. What a character. The great inventor was no quitter. And he had flair. Watch him shock an editor, a group of scientists, the president and the world with his newest invention.

Thomas Edison
at age 12 was selling candy
on railroad trains. As a young man
he showed his "talking machine"
at the White House.
Edison's boyhood home in Milan
is a museum today.

 Mr. Thomas Edison to see you, sir," the clerk told the editor.

The editor did not reply. He only sat, staring out the window, wondering, "What next?" He was the editor of the magazine *Scientific American*, and it was his duty to keep up with all the amazing new inventions that were popping up every day.

The world had just gotten used to steam engines and the telegraph. Then the railroad suddenly leaped from the Atlantic to the Pacific. Steel and oil industries were booming and now there was this new thing, the telephone.

It was all very exciting but it made your head swim, the editor thought. It was a comfort just to stare out the window. A gentle snow was dusting the buildings, trees and streets below, muffling the noise of New York City.

"Edison?" The editor had heard the name somewhere before.

"Shall I show him in, sir?" the clerk asked.

"Yes, yes—show him in," said the editor. He turned to find that young Mr. Edison had already entered. An inventor, the editor suddenly remembered. Yes, that was who this Edison was. Well, in that rumpled suit and with that brown-gray hair sticking out at all angles, he certainly looked the part. He was about thirty, pale and a little pudgy. And he was holding a rather big box.

Edison put the box down on the editor's desk. The two men shook hands as the editor said something.

"I beg your pardon, sir," said Edison, cupping his hand by his ear.

The visitor was hard of hearing. The editor repeated himself, louder this time. "I was guessing that you must have some new invention in that box," he said. Edison's eyebrows wiggled and a little smile crept across his face. "Oh yes, sir, indeed I do. You are about to become the very first person outside my workshop to see it."

That's what they all say, the editor thought. He felt like rolling his eyes, but he didn't. Many a so-called inventor had stood before him in this office. Every one was eager to show off the world's newest wonder. Most were crackpots, their inventions mere magic tricks. But there was something more to this Edison. Yes, now he remembered. Edison had improved the telegraph and also Alexander Bell's new telephone.

Edison opened the box and lifted out a strange device.

It was a machine of some kind, made of shiny metal. There was a crank at one end, a weight at the other and a strange-looking pair of round tubes in the center, set at right angles. The editor had no idea what the machine might do. He studied it closely.

"It's pretty enough," the editor said, trying to be polite. "But what does it do?"

Edison only lifted his finger, as if to say, Just you wait and see. The editor made a face. "This Edison is a showman," he thought to himself. "That's for sure."

Edison gave the crank a couple of turns. Then he let go and the crank began to turn, slowly, on its own power.

Without another word, Edison went out into the hall. He left the editor alone with the slowly moving crank handle. Suddenly, a thin, high VOICE began to rasp out of the machine. The machine was TALKING to the editor!

"May I ask, Mr. Editor," it said, "how is your health? And may I also ask what you think of me? I am called a phonograph. For myself, I am feeling quite well, thank you. But now I must bid you goodbye."

The editor's eyes grew wide and his mouth dropped open. The hairs rose on the back of his neck. He spread his sweating palms out flat on his desk and blinked his eyes rapidly.

A machine with a VOICE! But wait. Strange as it was, there was something he knew about that voice. It was Edison's! Was it a trick? Was Edison somehow "throwing" his voice from the hall? Was it a new kind of telephone?

Edison walked back into the office. The editor jumped to his feet and began pumping the inventor's hand.

"Astonishing, sir! Absolutely astonishing! What's the trick?"

"There's no trick to it, sir...." the inventor said. "The sounds are made by the aid of nothing other than the machine itself."

"Do you mean that this machine actually SPEAKS?"

"Well, it cannot create its own speeches, but the answer to your question is *yes*. The machine will speak back whatever words are spoken into it."

The clerk came back, saying, "Excuse me, sir, I couldn't help hearing...."

"Oh come in, come in," the editor said. "This must be seen–and heard–to be believed!"

The machine was made to repeat its little speech. Soon the entire staff of *Scientific American* was crowded into the office. They were amazed. It was as if Edison had shown them a flying carpet.

In fact, they would have been less amazed by a flying carpet. After all, they had all at least heard tales of flying carpets. But no one living in 1877 had even heard a story about a machine that could hear sounds and then repeat them.

Word spread through the building. Soon the office was so crowded that the editor feared the floor would collapse.

Four months later, Edison showed his invention to the National Academy of Sciences in Washington, D.C.

Once again, Edison made the machine speak for itself. "The Speaking Phonograph," it told the crowd, "has the honor of presenting itself to the Academy of Sciences." And when the machine repeated the singing, whistling and rooster crowing of Edison's helpers, several people in the audience fainted!

A friend of Edison's telephoned the White House. President Rutherford B. Hayes, of Fremont, Ohio, answered the phone himself. (In those days there were only about fifty telephones in Washington. The President liked to answer his calls in person.) Would the President like to see and hear Edison's amazing new talking machine? Hayes said he would.

So, just before midnight, Edison set the machine on the President's desk. When Hayes heard the thing speak, he was astounded. He woke up his wife so that she, too, could take in this new wonder. All the shouting, singing and rooster-crowing had to be repeated for the nation's leader and First Lady. Not until 3:30 a.m. was Edison allowed to leave.

In all Thomas Edison came up with more than a thousand inventions. But he always said that the phonograph was his favorite. It is strange to think that the phonograph was invented by a man who didn't hear very well. But maybe that's why it was his favorite invention.

Edison's little magic box grew into today's huge business of boom boxes, compact disks and radios.

And the recording industry is just one of many that grew from Edison's inventions. Think of movies. Edison invented the movie projector, the first movie studio, and film that could be wound onto a reel. Think of how our homes and streets are lit. Edison invented the light bulb. Think of all the electrical things we plug in. Edison invented the first central electric power station.

Edison was more than a scientist, more than an inventor. He was an explorer who had the courage to look for new continents where everyone believed none existed. He dared to imagine and create a whole new world of wonders.

The editor of *Scientific American* and the President of the United States were surprised. But just think how surprised the people must have been back in Milan, Ohio. Edison had lived there as a boy. Folks there knew he was quick and brave. They remembered him as the newspaper boy who risked his life to rescue a toddler who was playing in front of an on-coming train.

But the folks back home also remembered "Al" Edison as the worst student in the local school. They were amazed by his inventions and wondered, like everyone else, what was the secret of his success?

There was no secret, Edison snorted. Just work hard, stay with the job until it's done and, above all, *think*.

"Any other bright-minded fellow can do just as much," he said, "if he will stick to it and remember that nothing works by itself. You have got to MAKE the thing work!"

To learn more...

Edison's impact on our lives is so great that he sometimes is said to have "invented the Twentieth Century." You can read about him in many books, including *The Story of Thomas Alva Edison*, by Margaret Cousins (New York: Random House, 1997).

Edison's birthplace in Milan is maintained as a museum. Seven furnished rooms in an 1841 brick cottage exhibit some of his inventions and family possessions. Tel. (419) 499-2135. His Menlo Park, N.J., laboratory has been recreated at the Henry Ford Museum & Greenfield Village in Dearborn, Michigan. Edison lore can be found on the museum's web site: <http://www.hfmgv.org/>. Click on "Online Histories," then choose "Thomas Edison."

A sidelight: in Morrow County there is a tiny town named Edison, in honor of the great inventor.

11

The Black Edison:

Granville Woods
1856-1910

Reading and work. Are they a pain? Guess how this hero would answer. He's one who read and worked and learned his way to greatness.

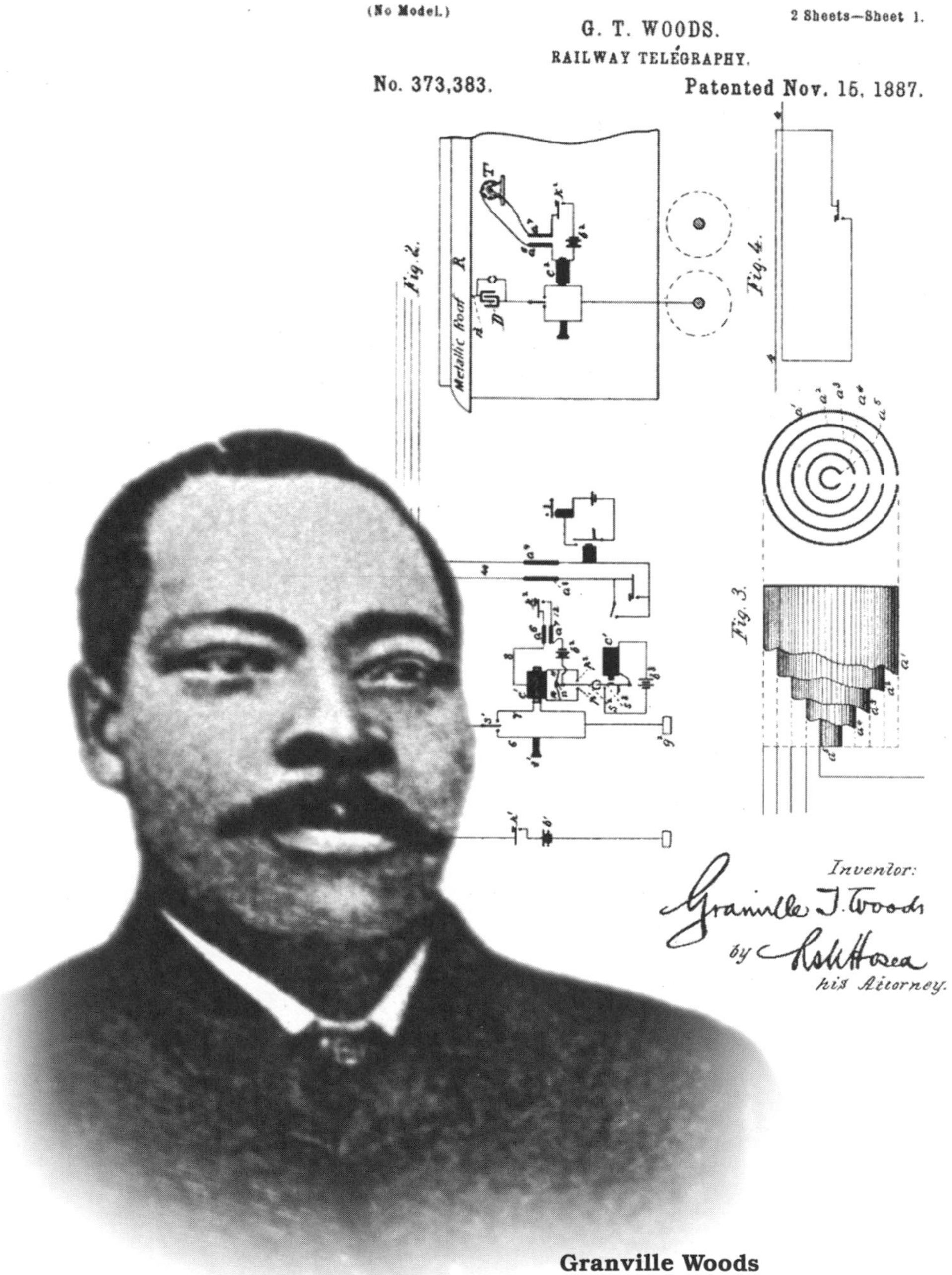

(No Model.)

G. T. WOODS.

RAILWAY TELÉGRAPHY.

No. 373,383.

2 Sheets—Sheet 1.

Patented Nov. 15, 1887.

Fig. 2.

Metallic Roof

Fig. 4.

Fig. 3.

Inventor:

Granville T. Woods

by Robt Hosea
his Attorney.

Granville Woods
was sometimes called
the "Black Edison." Just one of his
many inventions was a life-saving
railway telegraph system,
which he patented in 1887.

ranville Woods walked to the school building each morning. He carried a lunch bucket and had a book under his arm. He looked like any other 10-year-old African-American schoolboy in Columbus, Ohio.

But when he got to the school, he did not enter!

Granville Woods couldn't go to school. His family was too poor. He watched other kids enter the building. Then he walked on–to work. Granville had a job at a machine shop. All day he worked alongside blacksmiths and mechanics. When lunch time came, he opened his lunch bucket and his book. While he ate, he fed his mind–by reading.

Granville Woods was a boy with big plans. He meant to see the world and do big things. Granville knew that reading was the path that led to where he wanted to go.

Where did he get such ideas? Maybe from his name. Born in Columbus, he'd been given the name of a college town not far away. Granville. Maybe it gave him something to live up to. Maybe it reminded him to climb to higher and higher levels of learning...to keep on seeking until he knew all he needed to know. And then to give great gifts to the world.

For six years he worked in that shop. But he did more. He learned. He found work could be more than just a way to make money. A person could learn a lot by working. He mastered the secrets known to blacksmiths and mechanics. And he always carried a book to read at lunch time. This boy came to believe that learning-by-working-and-reading might even be the BEST way to learn.

All the while a bold plan was taking shape in his mind. He could not go to college. Instead, he would get the best education a person could get–from WORKING. He would work exactly two years each at one good job after another. Columbus offered few good jobs to African-Americans in the years after the Civil War, but that did not stop him. Young Granville would go where he needed to go.

At age sixteen he headed west. In Missouri he found a job as a fireman on a railway steam engine. Firemen tend the engine's fire. Granville grew strong by shoveling coal. He learned how engines worked and how to keep them running. He was so eager to learn that his bosses were amazed. They had never seen anyone like him.

Soon they promoted Granville to engineer—the engine's driver. He loved the chugging fury of the engines. Nothing was more exciting than guiding a great, black, puffing engine down the track at fifty miles per hour. He loved the breeze on his face and the way whole towns flew by.

It was risky work, though. He didn't dare read on the job. Melting snow sometimes washed out bridges. Storms sometimes sent mud slides or rock slides across the tracks. Branches could fall on the rails. An engineer had to be alert at all times.

The worst danger was other trains. A careless engineer might send trains crashing into each other, killing hundreds. Engineers never knew for sure if other trains were using the same track. Their only hope was to spot the headlight beam of an oncoming train. Or to hear another train's whistle above their own engine's roar. There was no other way for one train to signal to another.

Granville thought about that problem. At night, when the other railroad men were sleeping, Granville kept a lantern burning near his bed. He was reading books about an amazing force of nature–electricity.

Soon two years had passed. Granville loved the railroad, but he stuck to his plan: no more than two years on each job. At eighteen, he went to work in an Illinois steel mill. He soon learned how to mold white-hot liquid metal into all sorts of shapes.

All the while, he was borrowing books from friends, libraries and bosses. During every spare moment, at nights and on Sundays, Granville read everything he could find. Science, physics, math, magnets, new inventions and the lives of the great inventors. He gobbled up one book after another.

At twenty, he knew all he needed to know about *making* metal. What next? After metal is poured and molded, it has to be *shaped*. Very well, then. In New York City he found a job as a machinist. Sparks flew and the raw steel screamed as he shaped it the way he wanted.

Two years later it was time to move on again. As a boy he had dreamed of seeing the world. Now the time had come. At twenty-two he became an engineer on a British steamship. He tended the ship's engines as she crisscrossed the Seven Seas.

Granville saw terrible storms when the waves rose like mountains. He saw glassy calms when the ocean lay as still and smooth as a mirror. He saw vast icebergs made by the hand of Nature. He saw great cities made by human hands. He saw the trade of nations as ships were loaded and unloaded. And he learned all there was to know about ships' engines.

Again, his bosses took note. He soon became chief engineer. Still he read and read and read. The British sailors sometimes wondered about him.

"What is it those books be tellin' ye, mate?" they asked.

"They tell me how the world works," he answered.

"And why should ye be wantin' to know how the world works?" they asked again.

"So that I can change it," he replied, with a smile. This made the sailors laugh. But Granville wasn't joking.

At twenty-four, Granville returned to railroading. He would never stop learning the ideas of others. But now he began to hatch ideas of his own. He had found a way for engineers on moving trains to signal other moving trains. It was his amazing "Synchronous Multiplex Railway Telegraph." With electric signals from magnets placed near railroad tracks, moving trains could now send and get messages. No longer would engineers head blindly down the tracks looking for headlights or straining to hear whistles. Now they could be warned about bridges that were washed out, landslides, mud slides, fallen branches, and the locations of other trains. Hundreds, even thousands of lives would be saved.

Now Granville became a full-time inventor. He moved to Cincinnati and started the Woods Electric Company.

Three years later he gave the world his new Telephone Transmitter. It greatly improved the way telephones worked. Now people's voices sounded natural on the telephone. For the first time they could tell who was talking just by the sound of the voice they heard.

Other inventors began to hear of this African-American genius. Thomas Edison offered Woods a lot of money to come work for him. But Woods turned him down. He had worked for others already. He had been a success at each of his jobs. Now he wanted to work for himself.

He formed the Woods Railway Telegraph Company. It was a million-dollar company, a huge amount of money for that time.

Other inventions followed. Woods's new steam boiler furnace made ships and trains able to go farther with less fuel. His automatic air brake helped moving locomotives stop more quickly. If an engineer spotted cows crossing the track ahead, the brake gave him a better chance of stopping the train before it plowed through the herd.

In the days before automobiles most people got around cities on horse-drawn streetcars. Why not electric streetcars? Woods wondered. The problem was how to get electrical power to a moving streetcar. Granville drew on all he had learned from years of reading about electricity. And he drew on all he had learned from working at his many jobs. His learning made him ready to hatch an idea. It was simple, yet no one had thought of it. Fasten a metal pole on top of electric streetcars. Have the pole draw power from electrical lines overhead. It worked! Soon all the big city streets were hung with wires. Electric streetcars flew to and fro. Before long, Woods's idea was at work around the world. It paved the way for modern subway systems.

He even hatched an idea that helped hatch eggs. He found a way to use gentle electric heat to hatch chicken eggs.

And it was Granville Woods who perfected the electric model railroad, a toy that has delighted people ever since.

His inventions made life safer and easier and more fun.

Granville Woods' handsome face and black mustache became well known in Cincinnati. His work as a business owner and inventor won respect. An article in the Cincinnati newspaper of the time tells how scientists gathered to hear him speak on "the various laws and theories that pertain to electricity and magnetism."

Many called him "the black Edison."

Granville Woods was a self-taught, self-made hero.

Books and learning on the job were the secrets of his power.

To learn more...

The fascinating stories of many other creative African Americans are found in the book, *Created Equal: The Lives and Ideas of Black American Inventors*, by James Michael Brodie (New York: William Morrow, 1993).

Ohio boasts two museums of African-American lives and achievements. In Cleveland, the African American Museum is located at 1765 Crawford Ave.; telephone (216) 791-1700. In Wilberforce there is the National Afro-American Museum and Cultural Center, 1350 Brush Row Rd. Telephone (513) 376-4944.

A Web page about Granville Woods is one of many about African-American scientists to be found at <http://www.lib.LSU.edu/lib/chem/display/woods.html>. An excellent list of books can be found here, too.

12

They Wanted to Fly:

Orville, Katherine & Wilbur Wright

1871-1948, 1874-1929, 1867-1912

The Wrights weren't quitters. They were persistent, determined and daring. If something didn't work, they patiently figured out why not and then changed it. No wonder they finally flew.

The Wright Family's
first powered flight occurred in 1903.
Their achievements brought them
an invitation to the White House: (left to right)
Wilbur Wright, President William Howard Taft,
Orville Wright, Katherine Wright.

Eight strong men pushed and tugged the thing out of its long, narrow shed. It wasn't heavy. But it was wide and flimsy. They had to be careful. The thing was really little more than cloth stretched over thin slats of wood.

Six of the men were lifeguards. Not swimming pool lifeguards. These men rowed out to sea to rescue people from sinking ships. They fought the waves and howling winds that sometimes lashed the Carolina coast. They risked their lives to save others. They were heroes.

The other two men were brothers from Ohio. They were heroes, too, but of a different sort. They were quiet, patient heroes. They had built this cloth-and-wood thing. Built it from scratch, daring to experiment. And now they meant to make it fly.

A steady wind blew in the men's faces. It had a salty tang and it was cold. December is cold on the Carolina coast.

They said nothing as they pushed the flying machine along. The hiss of its skids slicing through the sand mixed with the purr of the surf and the cries of the seagulls.

The birds circled and glided above. Birds can glide a long time without flapping. Why can't people? It all began with that question.

Wilbur Wright and his brother Orville had always loved to figure out how things worked. Bicycles, for example. They made bicycles for the fun of it and sold them for money.

Making bicycles helped them think clearly about how people could fly. Looking at the problem as cyclists, they saw what everyone else had missed. When a bicycle leans, the cyclist puts a foot to the ground. When a glider tilts, the pilot cannot do that. The question was, how could a tilting glider get level again?

They had asked the right question. In science, that's half the battle. They quickly found the right answer. As Wilbur and Orville saw it, they had to make the "lift" of one wing stronger so that it would rise. And they had to make the "lift" of another wing weaker at the same time so that it would fall. Wings shaped right would do this. They made a new wing shape and tested it by building a large kite with two five-foot wings, one above the other. It worked.

Next? "We decided to experiment with a man-carrying machine...."

Orville later said. "We expected to fly...as a kite...able to stay in the air for hours at a time."

They couldn't fly an over-sized, kite-styled glider at home in Dayton, Ohio. Trees and buildings were in the way and the wind was always changing. They went to Kitty Hawk, North Carolina, where the wind was slow and steady. They pitched a tent and built another glider, this time with seventeen-foot wings.

Problems. They could not control the up-and-down motion. They made a rudder, like a ship's, and set it out front of the glider. The pilot controlled it with levers. Wind? They knew they could bicycle faster if they hunched over, out of the wind. So the pilot must lie on his stomach.

After a month of testing they went home to make new plans.

A year later they were back. They put up a larger tent and a wooden shed where they built their new glider. They were getting closer, but something was still wrong. The flow of air was hard to measure and to deal with.

Back home again they built a wind tunnel. A fan at one end blasted out a strong, steady breeze. In this wind they tested hundreds of model wings. Patiently, carefully, the two brothers measured the results. They found what shapes worked best. All the while they kept on making, selling and fixing bicycles for a living.

No one knew what they were up to. Only their family, the bicycle shop mechanic and a few lifeguards in Kitty Hawk. They kept their work a secret. No one believed that people could fly. The best minds had given up on the idea. Alone, day by day, the Wrights inched their way forward, learning Nature's laws of how air flows.

T heir sister Katherine helped. After their mother died, she became the female head of the family. She took over the household as her father's partner. When her brothers were away for months in North Carolina, she ran the bicycle shop. And she was an active feminist.

But she did more. Katherine gave the brothers a warm and friendly family. Inventing can be lonely work, but they were very close, Wilbur, Orville and Katherine. They cared more about each other than about anyone else.

Katherine gave the house over to her brothers' grand project. "Will spins the [sewing] machine around by the hour," she wrote to her father, "while Orv squats around marking the places to sew."

She also saw that her brothers were "growing thin and nervous." Yet, like them, she was sure of their success. And she knew that "they will be all right once they get down in the sand where the salt breezes blow."

Back at Kitty Hawk, the brothers glided hundreds of feet on a craft with 32-foot wings and a tail. They made hundreds of flights, including their best yet: a 600-foot, 26-second soar. They had licked the problem of control. They could build wings that worked. Their craft was strong enough to stand stiff winds and the shocks of rough landings.

Yet, when winter drove them away again, they felt discouraged. There was still so much they did not understand. Wilbur sighed and told his brother that a workable flying machine wouldn't be made in a thousand years.

Still, they kept on. Firm, practical, and daring, they took on one problem at a time. The craft needed power–a little engine with propellers that really worked.

No such engine had yet been built. So they set out to build one. They had never built a gas engine. But, well, they were the Wright Brothers. They had been tinkering almost since their baby days. Six months later, they had their engine. It had no cooling system and could only run for a minute. "Not much of anything," their mechanic said later, "but it worked."

Next they needed propellers. Again, they saw what no one else had: a propeller must work like a pair of wings whirling on an axle.

They made a new set of cloth-and-wood wings. This time the wings were 40 feet long.

Back at Kitty Hawk in 1903, Orville set a new world record with a glide of one minute, eleven seconds. The record was not broken again for another ten years.

But this time they planned to do more than glide. The engine was set in place beside the pilot. Two propellers were mounted. A simple chain-and-sprocket–like on a bicycle's–hitched the propellers to the engine.

Parts came loose; the weather turned mean. They passed rainy days tinkering with the engine. A propeller cracked and Orville had to dash back to Dayton to make another.

On the afternoon of Dec. 14, everything seemed ready. They tossed a coin for the first flight. Wilbur won. He climbed onto the machine. The engine was started, the propellers whirled, and down the track he went. The craft bobbed up...and humped down into the sand. The front rudder was crumpled.

Two days of repair. The weather turned bitterly cold. They had camped at Kitty Hawk for 84 days. All they had left to eat was canned beans. But the brothers were joyful. They knew they were going to fly.

Then came December 17, 1903. With the help of the lifeguards they dragged the machine to its track. It was Orville's turn. He gripped the levers. The racket of the engine scared away the seagulls.

The machine scooted down the track and rose into the air. It flew for just 12 seconds and only for about a hundred feet. You could throw a stone that far, easy. But it was enough. History had been made. For the first time, a machine had lifted human beings off the ground.

Wilbur took the next turn. Orville took another. Each flight was longer than the last. The final flight was almost a minute long and covered 852 feet.

Orville sent word to Katherine and their father back in Ohio: "Success! Four flights!"

Fame and fortune followed fast. Wilbur and Orville became the first heroes of the new century. The brothers did not forget their sister's help. She flew beside them when they showed off their flying machine in France. And she stood at their side as an equal when the Wright family was honored at the White House by President William Howard Taft.

Back at Kitty Hawk, the surf purred and the seagulls cried, the same as ever. But the world had changed. The Wrights had given people the gift of flight.

To learn more...

Two fine books for young readers are: Richard L. Taylor's *The First Flight: The Story of the Wright Brothers* (Danbury, Conn.: Franklin Watts, 1990) and Russell Freedman's *The Wright Brothers: How They Invented the Airplane* (Holiday House, 1991).

One of America's favorite tourist sites in Washington, D.C., is the National Air and Space Museum, where you can see the Wright's 1903 airplane. However, Ohioans are lucky: near Dayton is the world's largest and oldest air museum, the United States Air Force Museum. The museum has more than 300 aircraft and missiles, from the Wrights' own early aircraft, such as the 1911 Model B, through missiles used in the Persian Gulf War. Open all year; phone (937) 255-3286.

The museums are on the Web, too, with lots of good pictures: you can find the National Air and Space Museum (and lots of other great museums, too) at the Smithsonian Museum's Web site: <http://www.nasm.si.edu>. Find the Air Force Museum at <http://www.wpafb.af.mil/museum/index.htm/>. In Dayton, Carillon Historical Park offers 22 buildings, including one with the Wrights' 1905 Model III. Tel. (937) 293-2841. Park at <http://classicar.com/museums/carillon/carillon.htm>.

Liberator of Bulgaria:

Januarius MacGahan

1844-1878

Jan MacGahan drove himself to learn all he could. He was getting ready to do great things. Not even he could have guessed just how great those things would be.

Jan MacGahan
cut a dashing figure as a reporter.
He told the world about the horrors
of war in Bulgaria. A statue of the
"Champion of Bulgarian Freedom"
stands in New Lexington.

an MacGahan pressed his little pony along rough roads and up rugged paths into the beautiful mountains of Bulgaria. To MacGahan, the mountains looked a lot like the hills of Perry County back home in Ohio. He crossed over a mountain pass. Then he rode down into a patchwork of green fields striped by clear streams. Fields of golden corn and wheat made the gentle slopes look like checkered quilts.

But when he neared the fields, he noticed a strange thing. It was something that someone who had grown up on an Ohio farm would see right away. The corn was so ripe that the heavy ears had broken the stalks. Now they lay rotting on the ground.

Something else was wrong, too. At first he couldn't tell what it was. Except for the ruined corn, everything looked all right. Then it came to him. It was...the silence.

There were no sheep or cattle, nor any farmers. The only sound was the barking of a few wild dogs in the distance. Jan guided his pony toward them. The dogs were thin and in a fighting fury over meat they had found. One of them suddenly broke away from the rest, dragging something as the others chased after him. When the dog drew near, MacGahan could see the beast's awful prize.

It was a human head.

Jan MacGahan was a newspaper reporter and he had been sent to Bulgaria in search of a story. Bulgaria is a small country in Eastern Europe, not much bigger than Ohio.

MacGahan's boss was James Gordon Bennett, the best-known and toughest newspaper editor of the 19th-century. Bennett paid poorly and fired people left and right. But his papers sold by the millions.

MacGahan was Bennett's best man. Being a reporter came easily to MacGahan because he was curious about everything. As a boy he had studied the stars. As a teen he had buried himself in great books, history and math. As a young man he traveled around Europe. He had studied sword-fighting, riding and geography. When war broke out between Prussia and France, he got his first job as a reporter. The news stories he wrote about the war thrilled readers around the world. In fact, they made Bennett sit up and take notice. Here was a man who could write!

Before he was thirty, MacGahan had already seen more action than most men see in a long lifetime. Bullets had cut through MacGahan's hat. Bombshells bursting nearby had knocked him out cold. He had been captured and barely escaped firing squads in a Paris uprising. The same things happened to him again in a civil war in Spain.

He was the first outsider to cross Central Asia's deadliest desert. He marched with the Russian army into the ancient Moslem city of Khiva. He was the first American to get the highest honor Russia had to offer, the Order of St. Stanislaus.

He had married a beautiful Russian noblewoman but spent little time with her. He was too fond of adventure to stay home. He even journeyed as far away as the Arctic Circle.

Jan MacGahan constantly forced himself to learn. Soon it seemed he could do anything. He mastered NINE languages. He could ride like an Arab, sword-fight like a Frenchman and shoot like a cowboy.

But nothing had prepared him for the horrors he found in this peaceful Bulgarian valley.

For five hundred years the Turks had ruled the people of Bulgaria. Turkey was a much bigger country that lay southeast of Bulgaria. The Turks were very harsh rulers. Now the people of Bulgaria were asking for their freedom. The Turks answered them with savage cruelty.

The Bulgarian rebels filled MacGahan with wonder and sadness. They were brave, but how could they hope to win? Their army was small. Their soldiers were poorly dressed. The soldiers wore handmade wool uniforms and black fur hats. Their flag showed the lion of Bulgaria trampling on a Turkish crescent moon. Below this picture were the grim words, "Freedom or Death."

T he Turks laughed at the Bulgarians. Death was the Turks' only answer to the Bulgarians' pleas for freedom. Death, and rule by "yataghan," the cruel, curved Turkish sword. And the Turks sent Bulgaria the fearsome "Bashi-bazouks."

The "Bashi-bazouks" were soldiers famous for their cruelty. They rode into the quiet mountain villages of Bulgaria and dealt out death to everyone—men, women and children. By the hundreds, by the thousands! Many Bulgarian fathers even shot their own families and then themselves. It was better to die than fall into the hands of the terrible Bashi-bazouks.

The Bulgarians fought bravely, but it was no use. The Bashi-bazouks used tricks to win some of their battles. They promised mercy to the eight thousand townspeople of Batak if they would put down their weapons and open the gates. But when Batak surrendered, the Turks chopped off every head.

The outside world could not believe what was happening. People in Europe didn't think such things were possible. But they did not reckon with the Bashi-bazouks who knifed babies in front of their mothers.

At Batak, MacGahan saw hundreds of headless skeletons. Then he came to the worst sight of all: skulls stacked in heaps! Hundreds of human heads that had been laughing and praying only weeks before, cut off by the Turks and piled up like pumpkins.

Batak was now an empty ghost town, a city of the dead. Outside, the corn was rotting in the fields. The farmers lay dead in the streets.

Everywhere MacGahan went, he gave the Bulgarians a message of hope. He told them: "Before a year has passed, you shall see the soldiers of the Czar here to fight for your freedom!"

The Czar was the ruler of Russia, a huge country to the north of Bulgaria. The Russians thought of the Bulgarians as their cousins and wanted to help. But at first Great Britain, the most powerful country in those days, refused to let Russia help. The British Prime Minister read stories about the terrible deeds of the Bashi-bazouks, but he refused to believe them. He said such stories stretched the truth.

Then MacGahan began to write. He dashed off ten powerful news stories that boldly told what he had seen. These stories were better than the ones other reporters had written. MacGahan did what the best writers do: He looked for the facts. He was complete and accurate. He wrote clearly, in a way everyone could understand. And his writing was so vivid that it brought his scenes to life.

British newspaper readers were excited by MacGahan's powerful writing. Even Queen Victoria took note. And the Prime Minister lost his job for making light of the news from Bulgaria.

The new Prime Minister of Great Britain let Russia know Russia could come to the aid of her Bulgarian friends. Russia's troops got ready to attack the Turks. The Russo-Turkish War began.

MacGahan covered every detail of that war. His sharp words made readers see the Russian army crossing the Danube River. When Russian horsemen surprised the Turks in the mountain passes, MacGahan was there. He wrote down everything he saw and sent back the news.

The brave Bulgarians begged guns from the Russians and joined their army as it swept forward. It was a terrible war, like all wars. However, the Russians and their Bulgarian friends were winning it. At last the Turks raised the white flag of surrender. Bulgaria was free.

The rebels rejoiced—but their joy was soon cut short. The deadly winter of 1878 fell upon the weary country. Deep snow covered the land, and bitter cold gripped it. MacGahan did what he could to help. But everywhere he went, he found the frozen bodies of animals and people.

But to the Bulgarians who lived, MacGahan was the hero who had freed their country. Crowds flocked to see him. They kissed his hands, his bridle, his boots–even his horse! They called him their "savior" and "The Liberator of Bulgaria."

But then MacGahan's health began to fail. Even though he was ill himself, he went to care for a sick friend in a hospital. He even spent a whole night at his friend's bedside, trying to ease his chills. His friend had typhoid fever, a disease that comes from drinking dirty water.

MacGahan got sicker. His illness was worse than his friend's. He had typhus and nothing could save him. He died only few days before his 35th birthday.

The Bulgarians were deeply shocked by MacGahan's death. He had helped them win their freedom and now he was gone. Abraham Lincoln's death, thirteen years before, had made Americans feel much the same.

The Bulgarians made Januarius MacGahan's birthday–June 12– their national holiday. And that's how an Ohio farm boy who was curious about everything came to be remembered as "The Liberator of Bulgaria." Even today he is as great a hero to the people of that little Eastern European country as Abraham Lincoln is to us.

To learn more...

Januarius MacGahan: The Life and Campaigns of an American War Correspondent, by Dale Wallace (Athens, Ohio: Ohio University Press, 1988) is the only biography of the great war correspondent. However, chapters about MacGahan can be found in *Reporters at War*, by Alice Fleming (New York: Cowles, 1970) and *Famous War Correspondents*, by Frederick L. Bullard (New York: Beekman, 1974).

Information about Bulgaria, though little about its liberator, can be found on this World Wide Web site, *All About Bulgaria*: <http://www.cs.columbia.edu/~radev/bulgaria>. Studious books about Bulgaria include *A Concise History of Bulgaria* by R. J. Crampton (Cambridge: Cambridge University Press, 1997) and *A History of Bulgaria 1393-1885*, by Mercia MacDermott (New York: Praeger, 1962).

You can see MacGahan himself, bigger than life, by visiting New Lexington in southeastern Ohio. An impressive bronze statue stands there, across the street from the courthouse. A bust of the hero guards his gravesite in the New Lexington cemetery.

14

Little Sure Shot:

Annie Oakley
1860-1926

Heroes usually start out small, low and humble. Then they amaze us by climbing to great heights, one way or another. Phoebe Anne Mosey did it by shooting straight.

Annie Oakley
astounded the world with
her marksmanship in an age
when only men thought they knew
how to use a gun.

ANNIE OAKLEY

THE PEERLESS WING AND RIFLE SHOT

OAKLEY

The only beautiful thing in Susan Moses' sad and struggling home was her dead husband's handmade Kentucky rifle. It hung over the fireplace. The rifle had not been touched since the day Jacob had last shot game to feed his hungry family.

His tomboy daughter Phoebe Anne, whom everyone called Annie, had gone with him that day in 1865. It had been a fine, frosty October day. The kind of day when the sky is so blue it almost hurts your eyes, and the sun slices sharp shadows in the long grass.

Annie thought about that bright day a month later. She was waiting with the rest of her worried family for her father to come home. The sky had been gray and grim when he'd left. Soon it began to snow.

The family needed food but had no money. To get money, Jacob had to take their harvest of wheat and corn to the mill, fourteen miles away. The storm got worse, then turned into a blizzard.

The family waited. The hours passed, but they heard nothing beyond the cabin door but the howling wind.

Finally the wagon sounds came and the young mother opened the door—on a scene of horror. There stood the wagon, the horses at a standstill. And there sat Jacob, bolt upright, frozen stiff, the reins around his wrists and neck.

There was barely any life left in him. The doctor came but could do nothing. Jacob lingered through the winter. He died in the spring.

Now the widow and her six children had to take care of themselves. They worked long days tending the animals, farming the land, making their own clothing and storing food.

"But every night," Annie remembered much later, "no matter how tired we all were, mother washed our hands and feet. She brushed and plaited our hair into pigtails, took little John and Baby Huldie on her lap, and sang hymns with us and prayed God to watch over us."

Susan was a Quaker, strong in her faith and firm in her distrust of firearms. She noticed where little Annie gazed during the hymns. The seven-year-old girl couldn't keep her eyes off Jacob's rifle. By day its brass work glittered. By night its polished stock gleamed in the firelight. To Annie, it was a wondrous thing.

She yearned to hold the rifle, to aim it as her father had done, to point it at whatever things she wished, and then hit them.

Annie tried to think how she might help her family. There were squirrels, rabbits and game birds in the woods. She made traps from cornstalks and string, the way her father had taught her. Proudly she brought home game for her grateful family.

Still, Annie thought the traps were cruel to the little creatures. It was better to end an animal's life with a bullet, quick and clean. The beautiful Kentucky rifle above the fireplace beckoned to her.

One day, when Annie was eight years old, she "saw a squirrel run down over the grass in front of the house, through the orchard and stop on a fence to get a hickory nut." She dashed inside. She pushed a chair to the fireplace, climbed onto it and slid the rifle down.

The rifle was as long as she was tall, and heavier than she expected. She lugged it to the porch and stuffed it with enough powder "to kill off a buffalo." She balanced it on the railing and took aim. It was, she said, "my first shot, and I still consider it one of the best shots I ever made...a wonderful shot, going right through the [squirrel's] head."

Her horrified mother came running. She found the rifle leaning on the porch railing, smoke still rising from its barrel. Who could have fired it? A rustle of skirts and the sound of light footsteps prompted her to turn. There was Annie, a broad grin on her face, proudly holding the dead squirrel by the tail.

That's when Annie was given the gun to use as her own. Now she could roam the woods and fields of Darke County. She made every shot count, putting food for her loved ones on the table, just as Jacob had done.

Soon she was hunting wild game to sell to restaurants in Cincinnati. The restaurants knew their customers didn't like their meat pies filled with buckshot, so they paid Annie extra for game shot cleanly through the head. Annie could do that so well that she was able to earn enough money to take care of her whole family. She even made enough to pay back all the money her father had borrowed to buy the house.

Word of Annie's skill began to spread. A shooting match was set up with a marksman named Frank Butler. Butler earned his living by putting on shooting shows. Good as he was, though, Annie was better. She beat him in the shooting match.

Something even stranger happened next. Frank Butler and Annie fell in love and got married! Frank brought her into his act and then became her manager. They lived together happily all their lives, dying within a few days of each other in 1926.

Phoebe Anne Moses chose a superb stage name for herself: "Annie Oakley." The name fit her like a cowhand's glove. She had been a humble little acorn of a girl. Then she sprang to the strength of a young sapling...and finally to the grandeur of a full-grown oak.

The name is grand yet simple, strong and honest. It matches our idea of the Old West. It even sounds Western. Put "Oakley" after "Annie" and it's like the old cowboy yell, "Whoopee-tie-yie-yippie-yippie-oh!" Say it out loud: "Annie Oakley." It's "Yippie-oh!" with fringe and frills.

Annie Oakley became the star of the most popular act in show business, Buffalo Bill's Wild West. A famous American Indian, Chief Sitting Bull, saw the show and said Annie was the best part of all. He called her "Watanya Cecilla," meaning "Little Sure Shot."

Later the Chief himself became a part of the show for a time. He and Annie became good friends. Chief Sitting Bull was just one of many famous people who became her friend.

Annie even gave shows for the kings and queens of Europe. In her free time she went shooting with people like the Prince of Wales and the Grand Duke Michael of Russia. Queen Victoria of Great Britain told her, in her queenly way, "You are a very clever little girl."

Annie's trick shots were amazing. She would shoot the ash off a cigarette Frank held in his mouth. She could shoot a dime out of his fingers. She would leap over a table, pick up her rifle, then shoot out of the air two glass balls that had been tossed just as she began her jump.

She could fire left-handed or right-handed. She shot coins tossed in the air, split a playing card held edgewise, shot objects behind her by using a mirror. She could hit five targets thrown up at once, snuff out cigars and smash marbles.

When the bicycle craze swept the country, she quickly learned to ride one. Soon she was shooting live birds and glass balls from mid-air while wheeling in a circle, never touching the handlebars.

She had a few odd traits, as heroes do sometimes. When she missed a shot, which even she did once in a while, she would stamp her foot on the ground and pout. Then, when she made her shot, she would let fly with a little kick. That little kick became a trademark. Audiences loved to see her do it. When her act was finished, she'd take a bow, then run to the exit, doing her famous little kick one more time just before she vanished.

Annie became a superstar of her time, rich and famous. Even so, she stayed a proper lady, polite and kind. It was part of her image and it was the truth.

But Annie was also an athlete, a sport shooter and a hunter. In her day, those were thought to be things only men should do, never women. Yet, somehow, Annie was able to do manly things in a man's world while still acting like a lady. She combined sweetness and toughness in a manner all her own.

The "secret" of her success in shooting? "Nothing more simple," she once said. "Don't look at your gun. Simply follow the object with the end of it, as if the tip of the barrel was the point of your finger. But I'll tell you what. You must have your mind, your nerve and everything in harmony."

The secret of her success in life? "Aim at a high mark and you will hit it."

To learn more...

Among many books about Annie Oakley written for young readers are Robert Quackenbush's *Who's That Girl with the Gun? A Story of Annie Oakley* (New York: Prentice Hall Books for Young Readers, 1988) and Ellen Levine's *Ready, Aim, Fire! The Real Adventures of Annie Oakley* (New York: Scholastic, 1989). Glenda Riley wrote a scholarly study, *The Life and Legacy of Annie Oakley* (Norman: University of Oklahoma Press, 1994).

Many mementos of Annie's life (as well as many other historical relics) can be found in the Garst Museum, 205 North Broadway, Greenville, Ohio: (937) 548-5250. Don't miss Annie's statue in Greenville. And Greenville, Annie's hometown, is the scene of the Annie Oakley Festival late each July.

Only one short article about Annie Oakley, "The Real Annie Oakley," appears on the Worldwide Web: <http://www.maturityusa.com/Features/A.Oakley.html/>.

15

A Nickel and a Prayer:

Jane Edna Hunter

1882-1971

A rescue? Usually we think of a lifeguard pulling a drowning swimmer from the water. But there are other kinds of rescues, as Jane Edna Hunter's story shows.

Jane Hunter
worked tirelessly to help her people.
She grew up poor in the Deep South,
but came north to help others.
She built the Phillis Wheatley Association's
huge building in Cleveland.

Jane Edna Harris worried. Where was her friend? He said he'd meet her at the train station and pay for her ticket home. But now the train was whistling in the distance and she had no ticket.

She looked around her. Her fellow students were there. A few of them were fifteen years old like herself. Others were older. How happy their black faces looked! All had finished the school year at Ferguson & Williams College, a school for African-Americans in South Carolina.

It had been a good year for Jane. She had learned a lot in her classes. She had learned even more in her job as head of the college dining room. No one ever worked harder to do the job right. She later wrote, "There is always joy in the humblest household task for the worker who is proud of her position."

Jane also washed clothes for white families in town. In the 1890s this was an outdoors job, done by hand. In winter the wet clothes almost froze to her hands.

Even so, she earned very little. There was nothing left over for tickets home. Thank heavens for her friend—but where was he? As the train pulled up, she faced the bitter truth. He had broken his promise. She would be left behind. She burst into tears.

Word of her trouble spread among the others at the station. They passed the hat and soon it was sagging with the weight of nickels. She had her ticket with half a dollar to spare!

Most of these people were little better off than herself. Their kindness deeply touched Jane Harris. She made up her mind she "would someday do for others what these warmhearted souls had done for me."

Now she knew the power of the nickel, of many nickels gathered together. Now she knew not to believe everything a young man might say. These were the most useful lessons Jane learned during her first year at college.

In time, Jane finished school and became a nurse in Charleston, South Carolina. In spite of her quick mind and skillful hands, she was sometimes insulted because of her skin color. No matter; she just worked harder. She said that doing a good job was the best answer when a white person put her down.

Jane was briefly married to a man named Hunter. It was not a happy marriage, so they parted after only fifteen months. Even so, Jane kept the name Hunter.

Jane Edna Harris Hunter wanted to learn more, so she went to a school for nurses in Virginia. But it was hard there, too. At first she was only allowed to scrub floors. It was months before people saw how much more she could do. But when patients began to ask for "Nurse Hunter," she was sent to help the best doctors.

Then one day her white boss said Jane had done things that were wrong. It was a lie, but Jane was kicked out of the school.

She fled to the home of some friends who were about to go north to Ohio. All over the South, African-Americans were leaving farms for better-paying jobs in northern cities.

That was how twenty-three-year-old Jane Hunter came to Cleveland, full of "faith in God and hope for the future." She arrived with only $1.75 in her pocket. After long hours of walking and knocking on doors, she rented a small, dirty room in an old house. She had to pay $1.25 right away for a week's rent. Then she spent a quarter for a dinner of beef stew. That left her with only twenty-five cents. She had to find work fast.

"My search for lodgings," she later wrote, "gave me a keen insight into the conditions which confront the Negro girl who, friendless and alone, looks for a decent place to live."

Finding work was harder. One doctor told her to go back South. Whites did not hire "nigger" nurses, he said. "I am not a 'nigger'," was her reply. "If there are other nurses in Cleveland...I, too, can succeed."

Only a cousin's loan of ten dollars kept her going during those first weeks in the city. Finally a doctor hired her for a few days each week to give rubdowns to his patients. Other days, she cleaned houses and washed clothes. But there were days when she ate no more than "one raw egg, a plate of rice and a glass of milk." With no money for the bus, she often walked five miles to market to spend seventy-five cents on food.

After a year, though, Jane was a little better off. People saw that she was a good nurse. She earned a small but steady income. Yet she wanted to do more. She dreamed of doing something big and wonderful. She wanted to answer the voices of her people.

"The voices of my people!" she wrote. "Theirs is the music to which my life is attuned. The joys which they chanted are mine, and their sorrows. I was proud of the blood of my black ancestors. My life was to be a solemn dedication to the people of my mother's race!"

But what could she do? What did she have to give?

The answer came from a girl named Ruth. Ruth had come to Cleveland with her twin babies to get away from the shame she felt in Alabama. She was a mother without a husband. Jane helped her find a job with a family. But Ruth couldn't cook. She washed clothes badly. She broke things. Pretty but useless, she was fired. She was soon on the street with nothing but the clothes she wore and her babies.

She came to Jane, crying bitterly. Jane took her in.

"It was the old story," Jane wrote. "The young Negro girl pushed from the nest, alone and friendless in a northern city; reduced to starvation. It might easily have been my own story, had I been so poorly prepared to earn my living."

Then something clicked inside Jane Hunter. "It was borne in upon me that here was my work...here was the supreme task for which God had designed me." Jane's great task was to give girls like Ruth a home.

A month later, in September, 1911, Jane drew together her best friends. All were working women who had known many of the same troubles when they had first come to Cleveland. They remembered the lumpy beds and dim gas lights of rooms in old houses.

Jane explained her plan to her friends. "The Lord is going to help us to build a home for all the other poor motherless daughters of our race," she said.

That was how The Working Girls' Home Association began. Her friends chose Jane to be president of the club. They agreed that each member would pay a nickel each week. "We want this to be the work of poor people," she said, "and almost everyone can give a nickel." Each member agreed to bring ten more women to the next meeting.

The club grew quickly. Strangely, there were attacks from some other African-Americans. They said that Jane was wrong to make a home only for black women. The Negro churches worried that Jane's club was trying to take over their job. Newspapers wrote angry words.

Yet Jane's friends stuck together, and their enemies were won over, one by one. The group changed its name to the Phillis Wheatley Association. Phillis Wheatley had been an African-born Boston poet who, Jane said, "expressed in verse the upreachings of a free soul."

Fifteen months later, with $500 in hand, the Phillis Wheatley Association opened a house with rooms for ten young women. Soon, fifteen were living there. More houses were bought, then a big building with room for seventy-five.

By 1927, after raising half a million dollars, the Association opened the brand-new, nine-story Phillis Wheatley building. There was room for a hundred women.

The Phillis Wheatley project did so well that it became a model for other cities. Jane Hunter gave the rest of her life to leading the group she had founded. Sometimes her work led her into bars and rough places to rescue poor girls. Other times she found herself honored at colleges. When she felt she needed to know more about law, she earned a law degree from Marshall University. She became a leader of her people.

"There is a great force in the bodies, minds and hearts of Negro citizens," she said. "Too long this energy has been overlooked. It is the mission of the Phillis Wheatley Association to discover and protect the beauty and power of Negro womanhood."

"It is the 'Promised Land' for which we must work together, children!"

Jane Edna Harris Hunter died in 1971, but the work of the Phillis Wheatley Association goes on today.

To learn more...

Jane Edna Hunter told her own story in *A Nickel and a Prayer* (Cleveland: Ellia Kani, 1940). The book includes a photograph of her humble birthplace in South Carolina. More recently, Adrienne Lash Jones wrote a studious book about her life: *Jane Edna Hunter: A Case Study of Black Leadership, 1910-1950.* (Brooklyn, N.Y.: Carlson, 1990). One in the series *Black Women in the United States*, the Jones book includes a chapter on the history of Black Cleveland and several photographs of Jane Edna Hunter and the Phillis Wheatley Association. The Phillis Wheatley Association continues its work today, through day care, summer camps and services to the elderly, at 4450 Cedar Ave., Cleveland; tel. (216) 391-4443.

The African American Museum, 1765 Crawford Rd., Cleveland, has interesting exhibits and presentations. Tel. (216) 791-1700.

16

Parade in the Rain:

Elizabeth Hauser
1873-1958

*Rights are not handed out. People must fight for them.
If women had waited quietly to be allowed to vote,
they'd still be waiting. Elizabeth Hauser was not
content to wait.*

Elizabeth Hauser
believed women should be able
to vote. She and her friends used riders
on horseback, parades and lots of signs
to trumpet their cause.

ABOOM! Thunder, lightning, howling wind, pounding rain. This was not the weather the Republicans wanted for their June convention in Chicago. And now there was another sound as well–the jangle of...music!

The storm had roared all day. By 4 p.m., the daytime work of the convention was over. The Republicans—all men—had returned through the rainy streets to their hotel rooms. They were drying out and resting before dinner when they heard that music. Looking out their windows, the men were stunned to see a moving army of bobbing umbrellas. Thousands of women were marching!

Many of the men went downstairs to watch. No fewer than 10,000 women were marching through the downpour, along with twenty-two marching bands. There were even *elephants* marching with the women!

One of those women was Elizabeth Hauser of Girard, Ohio. She and the other marchers wanted something that American women did not have and that many wanted very much. American women wanted the right to vote...a right they had never had. The parade in the rain was meant to show the country that America belonged to ALL the people, not just men.

Today, women have the same voting rights as men. It may be hard to believe that was not always true. But in 1916, voting to choose the nation's leaders was one of the things women could not do.

Elizabeth was a newspaper reporter. That was unusual. In those days few women worked outside the home. She wrote stories for Cleveland newspapers. She never married. She gave her whole heart to her work, to her sister's children, and to winning for women the right to vote.

It looked as if 1916 could be a big year for her favorite cause. At their national conventions the Republicans and Democrats would decide on their "platforms"—where they stood on important questions.

For more than half a century, leading women had asked for the right to vote. They were called "suffragettes" because they wanted "suffrage." That's a fancy word for the right to vote. These women had formed a national club. Each year they made careful plans to try to win over both parties. Some men were on their side. In every state the women pressed them to do all they could to help.

In Ohio, Elizabeth Hauser and her helpers got many leaders to promise they would try to pass a law to let women vote. Elizabeth went up and down the state, speaking at picnics and club meetings. She got more and more women to join her. Slowly and steadily she formed Ohio women into a strong force. She even took on the job of winning over Ohio's newspaper bosses. Many came out for women's right to vote, but some were against the idea.

But the real battle would take place when the Republican and Democratic national conventions met. Elizabeth Hauser met with other women leaders to make plans. The women planned to put on a huge parade when the Republicans met in Chicago the second week of June. Ten thousand women would march through the streets to the big hall where the Republicans would meet.

It was a grand plan, and Elizabeth was excited.

Thousands of women arrived in Chicago days ahead of the parade. They made banners, hired marching bands, and printed the words "Votes for Women" on the yellow ribbons they always wore. To make the Republicans stop and think, the women even got some elephants from a local zoo to join them in the parade. Since the elephant is the sign of the Republican Party, the women hoped the Republicans would pay attention

A small group of the Republicans were given the job of listening to both sides of the votes-for-women question. This group would then tell the rest of the Republicans whether to be for or against letting women vote.

Many men thought women should not vote. They said women did not know enough to vote and should think about their families instead. Strangely, even some women did not want the right to vote. They thought that they already had enough power when they told their husbands, fathers, brothers and sons how they felt about things. Why did they need to vote?

The leader of the women against voting was Alice Chittenden. She spoke first to the Republicans. She said that they should not seek votes for women. The idea stirred up people, she said, "and the times were too serious for political parties to take up such matters." Then Elizabeth Hauser and others spoke up. They reminded the men that women were Americans, too. They said that if women paid taxes, then they should have the right to vote.

Meanwhile, thousands of women waited in the streets. Their yellow ribbons showed they wanted the right to vote. They wondered what the small group would decide. They begged to be let inside but were not allowed to enter.

The meeting went on and on. Finally, the small group of Republicans made their decision. It was not good news for the women who wanted to vote. The decision was to tell the Republican Party not to take any stand at all on the question of votes for women.

This was a serious blow. The women's last hope was to change the Republicans' minds with the big parade planned for the next day.

But then the weather turned very bad. Floods of rain fell from a gray sky and a biting wind blew through the streets. The women had expected warm and sunny June weather. They had brought only light, summer clothes. That June morning felt more like March, or even February.

The women tried to decide what to do. The weather was so bad that many felt there could be no parade. Some of the women were old and weak. Some felt that real ladies should not march in parades at all, even in nice weather. Many nodded in agreement. Marching in a cold and windy rain storm seemed downright crazy.

Others felt that it was now or never. If the Republicans didn't join their cause, neither would the Democrats and the idea would stay stuck. A parade just might win over the Republicans. Elizabeth Hauser listened as the wind moaned at the windows and the rain drummed on the roof.

Finally, one woman said something that made them all stop and think. We will never know who she was, because the newspaper stories don't tell us her name. But perhaps it was Elizabeth Hauser. She rose and looked into the ladies' worried faces. Then she simply asked, "If you ever have the vote, you expect to vote on RAINY days, don't you?"

That settled it! The women burst into applause. The parade was on. It would begin at 4 p.m., as planned. The excited women spent the day getting ready, buying every umbrella and raincoat in town.

Then the women lined up in rows and columns, filling block after block of city streets. When the signal was given, the bands struck up and the gathered thousands of women surged forward.

The newspapers called it "the strangest parade that ever went through the streets of Chicago." The marchers were soon soaking wet. Their raincoats and umbrellas weren't much good against the winds whipping about them. Some of the women were nearly blown over as they struggled along carrying sticks with big, yellow banners stretched between them. "Votes For Women!" the banners demanded. Yellow ribbons with the same words stuck to their wet clothes. Surely the women were cold and wet. But every one wore a big smile.

There was something funny, yet stirring, about this parade. The Republicans were touched when they saw the marchers plodding bravely through the storm. Even the elephants were shivering. Some of the Republicans told reporters that it was "the pluckiest thing they had ever known women to do." Others said that "parades on clear days would not have done half so much to convince us."

The parade ended at the convention hall. There Elizabeth Hauser and the other leaders gave the Republicans a slippery, wet board—a "plank" for the party platform. On this piece of wood were the words of a law that would give women the right to vote.

The women who were against the idea were also there. They had come by automobile. They stood to one side, comfortable and dry. Maybe they felt a little ashamed standing next to those women who had dared to march through the storm.

The next day the Republicans decided to back a law giving women the right to vote. A week later the Democrats did the same.

The new law took four more years to pass. But Elizabeth Hauser and all the other brave women who marched in the famous "Parade in the Rain" finally reached their goal. In 1920 American women won the right to vote.

To learn more...

Elizabeth Hauser was just one of many who fought for women's rights. An enjoyable story about a little girl who grew up to be another one of the leaders is told in *You Want Women to Vote, Lizzie Stanton?* by Jean Fritz (New York: G.P. Putnam's Sons, 1995). Another good book for young readers is *Petticoat Politics: How American Women Won the Right to Vote*, by Doris Faber (New York: Lothrop, Lee and Shepard, Inc., 1967).

Two careful studies of the movement's history are found in Eleanor Flexner's *Century of Struggle: The Woman's Rights Movement in the United States* (Cambridge: Belknap, 1975) and Doris Stevens' *Jailed for Freedom: American Women Win the Right to Vote* (Troutdale, Oregon: NewSage Press, 1995).

The League of Women Voters, founded in 1920, is nonpartisan. Useful information can be found on its web site <http://www.lwv.org>, including links to several web sites of Ohio chapters of the League. A brief biography and picture of Hauser can be found at <http://www.state.oh.us/obes/HAUS.htm#1>.

For many years Elizabeth Hauser was secretary to Harriet Taylor Upton, whose home at 380 Mahoning Ave., NW, in Warren served as national headquarters for the Women's Suffrage Association. For speakers or tours of the home, call the Fine Arts Council at (330) 399-1212.

17

He Beat the Nazis:

Jesse Owens
1915-1980

Many call Jesse Owens the greatest sports hero ever. Why? Not just because he was the best. But also because he was modest, played fair and proved the haters wrong.

Jesse Owens
was usually seen in running
shorts —and moving *very* fast.
In late August, 1936, however,
Jesse dressed up in a suit as
he returned to America in triumph,
the winner of four gold medals
in the Berlin Olympics.

Firom under the gleaming brim
of his military hat, Adolph Hitler's dark eyes swept the stadium. It was
the largest ever built. One hundred and ten thousand seats and all of
them filled. His jackboots clicked and his little mustache bristled with
pride. Red and black Nazi banners hung everywhere. A band played a
jangling march. Hitler's sneering lips twisted into a grim smile. The day
of triumph had come at last, he thought.

These were the Olympic Games of 1936. They were being held in
Berlin, Germany, the nation Hitler and his Nazis ruled. This was Hitler's
chance to show the world that the white people of northern Europe were
the best at everything.

Sure enough, the first two gold medals went to Germans. Hitler
greeted his athletes with glee. He shook their hands and posed with them
for newspaper photos. Things were going just as Hitler had planned.

Then a young African-American athlete from Cleveland entered the
stadium. He was the tenth child of a dirt-poor farmer. His grandparents
had been slaves. His name was Jesse Owens.

Hitler's eyes narrowed. The smile left his lips. He clasped his hands
behind his back and leaned forward to watch.

History was about to be made. Hitler thought he knew how. His white
Germans would clip this black sprout. His Nazi athletes would win all
the gold medals.

At the time, that seemed likely.

Today, there are many African-American athletes. We know their
worth and we admire them. But not so long ago things were very
different. In 1936 there was not a single African-American player on any
professional sports team. Not one. And there were hardly any African-
Americans on college teams.

Why not? Racism. Hitler and his Nazis were not the only ones who
believed whites were best. Millions of Americans also believed it then.

But then came Joe Lewis. He became the first African-American
boxing champion of the world. When they heard the news, millions of
black Americans whooped with joy. Finally, one of their own people had
shown the world that a black man could be "the best."

Next came Jesse Owens. The handsome young athlete was coming
to the Olympics with a winning record. He had been a track star for Ohio

State University. But what he had done at a track meet in Ann Arbor, Michigan, not long before, had spread his fame around the world.

Owens had gone to Ann Arbor with a stiff, sore back. A few days, before he had slipped on a stairway and hurt himself. Luckily, that day in Ann Arbor was warm and bright. And maybe Jesse's pain helped him to think hard on what he had to do. That day he was perfect. "My knees were working perfectly," he said. "My arms were...with my legs. The body position that we worked so hard for was there." Note that word "we." It shows Jesse sharing the glory with his coaches.

What did he do that day? He did something no one had ever heard of. He ran so well that he broke THREE world records—and tied another—in less than sixty minutes!

A Cleveland reporter caught the moment: "The 12,000 spectators were stunned into silence and then moved to tremendous...applause when the Buckeye ace staged his almost unbelievable show."

Many still call that day in Ann Arbor the greatest in the history of track. After it, Jesse Owens and Joe Lewis shared the spotlight as champions. Then Joe Lewis got beat. Now Jesse was left alone to carry the hopes of African-Americans to the Olympics. But the games were being held in Germany. And it was a German who had beaten Joe Lewis! To some, it seemed to prove that white people were the best after all.

Still, many put all their hopes in Jesse Owens.

And not just black Americans. In 1936 America felt almost hopeless. It was a hard time. There were no jobs. Millions of Americans were poor, even starving. Many other countries thought America was failing. The Germans put aside their freedoms and gave unlimited power to Hitler. Democracy had failed in China. And Russia had gone Communist.

America needed to prove itself. The Land of the Free badly needed an Olympic hero. If the son of a poor black farmer in America could go up against the world's best athletes and win, then maybe America wasn't failing after all.

On the ship going to Germany, Jesse wondered how he would be treated at the games. He knew how he would treat others. Fairly and with friendly respect. When he got there, he smiled and shook hands with everyone. They smiled back. Even some German athletes liked him and one even became a good friend.

Jesse Owens won respect wherever he went. Not just by breaking records. He played fair. One time, a few years before, he had to race on a badly made track. When the starting gun was fired and the runners burst forward, one of them, named Eulace Peacock, stumbled. His starting block had slipped. When Peacock got back his balance, he was so far behind that he quit the race. Jesse ran ahead to an easy victory. But when Jesse learned what had happened, he demanded that the race be run again. This time Jesse finished inches BEHIND Peacock. He lost that day's race, but he won the respect of everyone there by playing fair.

S o when Jesse entered Germany's Olympic stadium, he brought with him fame as a runner and as a sportsman. And he brought more. That day he carried the hopes of a people and a nation. A black man, he brought those hopes into a Germany that was teeming with racial hatred. The strain of all this might have crumpled a lesser man. Jesse shrugged it off. He simply made up his mind to do his best.

The record books tell what happened. No track-and-field athlete had won three gold medals in a single Olympics since 1900. But now, in Berlin, in the face of Nazi racism, Jesse won *three* gold medals. Then he went on to do something no one had ever done before. To Hitler's fury and the amazement of the world, Jesse Owens won a FOURTH.

None of the records he set that day were beaten until the 1950s. His long-jump record lasted for 24 years, until 1960. No other track-and-field athlete snagged as many gold medals until 1984.

Jesse Owens may well have been the greatest Olympic athlete, not just of his time but of all time. We'll never know. Things were so different then. In Jesse's day, Olympic runners did not use starting blocks. Instead, they were given little shovels to dig a trench for their feet! Today's athletes run on smooth, man-made tracks. Jesse had to run on wet cinders. His leather running shoes were much heavier than today's high-tech, feather-light shoes. His shoes got even heavier after soaking up rain water from the cinders. Even with these drawbacks, his running times were astonishing.

From his seat among his generals, Hitler saw it all. There was no way to deny Jesse Owens his victories. He had defeated the best white athletes of Hitler's Nazi Germany, the same people who called themselves "The Master Race." These people claimed their race was better than any other. All by himself, Jesse Owens had shown the world that such an idea was nonsense.

No wonder Hitler was angry. He turned away. His generals turned with him. They left the stadium. Hitler would not shake hands with black athletes, even if they had won fairly. He returned in the days that followed. But he would shake no more hands. There would be no more photos for the newspapers. Filled with hate, Hitler would rather shake no one's hand than have to shake hands with a black athlete.

Jesse's thoughts? "We weren't there to worry about Hitler," he said. "There were six of us finalists [for the 100 meter dash]...yet there could only be one winner. Why worry about Hitler?"

Hitler had come to the games filled with hatred. Hatred for people different from himself. Owens had come filled with love. Love for his country, for his people, for sports and for running.

"I always loved running," he said, much later. "I wasn't very good at it, but I loved it because it was something you could do all by yourself and under your own power. You could go in any direction, fast or slow as you wanted, fighting the wind if you felt like it, seeking out new sights just on the strength of your feet and the courage of your lungs."

That's worth reading again. It's pure Jesse Owens, modest yet noble. Not very good at running? By running, this athlete left the greatest legacy any Olympic athlete has ever left. Not only did he set records, he dared to set them in the face of hatred–and prove the haters wrong.

To learn more...

Jesse Owens: An American Life by William Joseph Baker (New York: Free Press, 1988) is "a powerful biography of an athlete who never lost his dignity," one reviewer wrote.

The Jesse Owens Official Site, including a photo gallery, can be found on the World Wide Web at <http://www.cmgww.com>. Click on "Sports," then "Other Sports Legends" to find Owens.

A monument to Jesse Owens stands at the entrance to the stadium at Ohio State University in Columbus, where Jesse was a star athlete.

18

Little Man, Big Hero:

Rodger Young
1918-1943

Are heroes like movie stars? Rodger Young wasn't. He didn't see well. He didn't hear well. And he was short. But to those who knew him, he was a giant.

Rodger Young
was given a hero's burial
in the town of Clyde.
He died fighting to save his comrades.
A Medal of Honor is engraved
on his headstone.

I t was a high pop, flying deep into center field. Don't worry. Rodger Young was there. He leaped up, snatched the ball from the air, and then snapped it to third base for a double play.

The quarterback fumbled, the football squirting out from under his elbow. No cause for alarm. Rodger scooped it up and made fifteen more yards before he was tackled. Glory! Even if it was just a backyard game.

The crowd gasped as the ball soared toward the basket–and then bounced off the hoop. Not a problem. Rodger caught the rebound. As the crowd cheered, he dribbled fast to half-court. Then he passed the ball to a teammate who scored.

Rodger Young was a short guy. He wasn't the best player on any of his high school teams–not by a long shot. But all the other players respected him. They knew they could count on him. There was no other young man like him in Green Springs, Ohio. His high spirits always fired up his teammates. His hope for victory spread through the team, the coaches, the fans. That meant a lot in the 1930s, when times were tough for everyone.

Too small to make the high school football team, he played in backyards every chance he got. He put the rest of his energy into baseball and basketball.

And it was basketball that nearly destroyed him. Ball in hand, he jumped high to make a long shot. Then a player on the other team clipped his legs out from under him. "Foul," roared the crowd as Rodger fell, banging his head with a sickening thud on the shiny hardwood floor. The sounds and the lights dimmed as Rodger sank into a gray and untroubled sleep.

When he opened his eyes, the crowds were nowhere to be heard or seen. And he wasn't on a gym floor–he was in a hospital bed. His parents and his older brother were there, at his side, and the doctor, too. "He's come to!" the doctor said, and everyone smiled.

Rodger left the hospital for home that same night. The doctor said he was OK, but he didn't feel right. His head hurt and it was harder to hear. In a few months, his eyes went bad and he began wearing glasses.

He couldn't play sports anymore. It was hard for Rodger to hear what his teachers said or to see what they wrote on blackboards.

So Rodger dropped out of high school and went to work in a factory. He still loved sports and sports news. The amazing things sports stars did with baseballs, footballs and basketballs made Rodger's heart beat fast.

To earn extra money, Rodger and his brother joined the National Guard. Then a year later, World War II broke out. The two brothers got orders to join the regular army.

The training was tough but Rodger liked being back on a team again. He ate it up. By the time he sailed off to join the action in the Pacific, Rodger had been promoted to the rank of sergeant. He was in charge of a rifle squad. Even with bad eyes and poor hearing, his high spirits and hard work made him a leader. His men respected him and knew they could count on him.

Rodger was very proud of his sergeant's stripes. He worked as hard as he could to get his men ready for battle. But he knew that his hearing was getting worse. It was a problem he could not ignore. What if, when he and his men reached the war zone, he failed to hear the telltale snap of a twig in the jungle? Missing that sign might cause his men to fall into an enemy trap.

So he made one of the hardest choices of his life: He gave up being a sergeant. Instead, he asked to be reduced to the rank of private. Rodger's commander was sorry to give him his way on this, but he knew it was the wise thing to do. A private once more, Rodger was happy when he found he would still be with his old squad.

The time for combat had come. Fighting in the South Pacific, the American Army and Navy were taking territory from the Japanese an inch at a time. In the summer of 1943 Rodger Young's unit arrived on the island of New Georgia. The Americans were trying to capture an enemy airfield on the southwestern tip of the island.

Capturing the airfield was very important. But it also was very hard. The American soldiers had to fight their way through thick jungles. It rained nearly every day. There were deep-running streams and dangerous swamps. The heat and mosquitoes were terrible. The enemy soldiers were far worse.

The Japanese had built careful defenses around the airfield, hiding guns in trenches five feet deep. They piled logs in front of the trenches and hid them with palm branches. Snipers and night raiders attacked the Americans again and again. The attack slowed to a halt.

Then, on July 31, 1943, the Americans made a wide sweep through the jungle and came up behind the Japanese lines. They were only a thousand yards from the airfield when the Japanese attacked and cut them off. The men in Private Rodger Young's squad tried to get back to their own lines but bullets rained down on them from a well-placed Japanese machine gun.

Rodger Young and his men were trapped. One by one, the enemy fire was cutting them down. The worst part was that the Americans could not even see where the machine gun nest was. Something had to be done or the whole squad would be wiped out.

Lying on his belly in the mud, Rodger Young squinted through his glasses, trying to see through the thick jungle. Suddenly, just seventy-five yards away, he spotted a spurt of orange flame. The machine gun was firing right at him! A crushing blow thumped into his shoulder.

Young's eyes never left the spot from which that orange flame had come. He began crawling forward. A buddy yelled to him, "You're hit!"

"Yes, but I see the machine gun!" he yelled as he crawled through the brush, leaving behind him a bright trail of blood on the yellow-green jungle floor.

"Rodger, come back!" the soldier called. Maybe Young's bad ears didn't hear. Or maybe he had already decided what he was going to do.

Shoulder throbbing, he wormed his way through the mud. Every ten feet or so, he fired off a few shots and then kept on creeping closer. The rest of the squad, realizing what he was trying to do, kept up a hail of fire at the enemy gun, trying to cover Young's one-man attack.

Rodger Young had pulled himself to within fifteen yards of the enemy when they spotted him. Aiming the machine gun at him, the Japanese let fly a hale of bullets. Young shook as the hot rounds ripped into him.

Don't worry. Rodger Young was there. He snatched a grenade from his halter and snapped it toward the machine gun nest.

Young fumbled in the mud, the blood squirting out from under his elbow. No cause for alarm. He scooped up another grenade and tossed it, too. Glory! And this was no backyard game.

There was no crowd to gasp as his third grenade soared toward the enemy. Not a problem. Rodger was dribbling blood fast now. Winning the airfield would have to be passed to his teammates.

The sounds and the sunlight dimmed as Rodger sank into a gray and untroubled sleep.

The machine-gun nest was destroyed by the grenades the badly wounded private from Ohio had thrown. The trap had been sprung. Rodger Young's squad escaped and, thanks to him, lived to fight on.

But Rodger Young himself was dead.

Shortly after, the airfield was captured. Within a few days American airplanes were landing and taking off there, pushing the war ever closer toward Japan. The Americans knew that victory would come one day.

He was a short guy with glasses who didn't hear very well...but his bravery earned him America's highest military honor. Back in Ohio, on January 17, 1944, the parents of Rodger Young were presented with his Medal of Honor, given to them in his memory.

To learn more...

The story of Rodger Young, as well as many other heroes, can be found in *Heroes of World War II* by Edward F. Murphy (Novato, California: Presidio, 1990). The book has a chapter on the history of the Medal of Honor which also mentions the Ohio heroes of the Civil War's "Great Locomotive Chase."

Rodger Young's gravestone may be visited in the McPherson Cemetery, at the intersection of Routes 20 and 101 in Clyde.

For the full text of Rodger young's Medal of Honor citation, go to World Wide Web address <http://160.147.68.21:80/cmh-pg/mohiib.htm/>. *The Interactive Guide to World War II* is on the Web at http://tqd.advanced.org/10494/. The sights and sounds of World War II can be found here.

19

More Head Than Heels:

Emma Gatewood
1888-1973

Suppose people said you couldn't go on the biggest adventure of your life because you were the wrong sex or the wrong age. Would you go anyway? Emma Gatewood did.

Emma Gatewood may have been a grandmother —but she wasn't afraid of going hiking where no woman had gone alone before.

queer little voice, shrill and silly, floats above the rush of raindrops falling on the mountain side. It rises from the dark green forest. It draws quickly near. Is it cackling, crackling or crying? Wait, there are words ... and a tune. An old woman is singing a hymn:

There shall be showers of blessing
Precious reviving again
Over the hills and the valleys
Sound of abundance of rain.

Friendly, she waves her walking stick at us. The teeth in her smile are like little white stones, her face brown as a log. She's just over five feet tall and just under seventy years old.

She wears a shower curtain for a rain coat. Her flannel shirt hangs out over her baggy pants. Her sleeves are rolled up and her arms are as tan as her face. A homemade cloth sack is slung over her shoulder. In it she carries barely fifteen pounds of food and gear. All she needs to live in the wilderness.

No partners, no map, no guidebooks, no sleeping bag, no tent, no regular backpack. She doesn't wear boots, only a pair of soggy sneakers.

Who is she and what is she doing?

Her name is Emma Rowena Caldwell. She was born in Mercerville, Ohio, in 1887. She was one of 15 children. Her grandparents were pioneers. She married Perry Gatewood when she was 19. She raised four sons and seven daughters on a worn-out little farm near the West Virginia and Kentucky borders. She hoed corn, pitched hay, chopped tobacco. She cleaned other people's houses for extra money.

Time flew. One day, after her children were grown, she read a magazine article about the world's longest footpath. It ran for 2,100 miles across the tops of the mountains all the way from Georgia to Katahdin, a mountain in Maine. The footpath was called the Appalachian Trail. She decided to hike it. The whole thing. At the age of 68.

She didn't know a thing about hiking. She knew she'd make mistakes. She figured she'd learn as she went. July found her at Mount Katahdin, setting off to hike down the trail from the north. Mother Nature quickly showed her that this was her first mistake. "The blackflies nearly ate me up," she said.

Worse mistakes soon followed. To stay on the trail, hikers must follow white paint marks on trees and rocks. She didn't know this and soon lost her way. After three very rough days she came to a lake and a party of forest rangers who had been looking for her. "Welcome to Rainbow Lake," one ranger said. "You've been lost."

"Not lost," Emma chirped back, "just misplaced."

Most people would have quit right then. Not Emma Gatewood. She took a bus to Georgia and started out again, heading north. This way she would miss the blackfly season. "I figured by the time I got to Maine, it would be cold, and their tails would freeze off," she said.

There were many other lessons to learn. Stinging nettles taught her that pants were better than a skirt. Light as she traveled, she found there were things she didn't need. "A sudden hailstorm took my cap sailing round the mountain, whipped my raincoat from my hand and knocked me flat.... I lost my cap...and just never bothered to get another."

Hiking alone worked best. She could move at her own speed, setting out at dawn, stopping in the late afternoon.

She slipped and fell hundreds of times. But she wouldn't wear leather boots. They gave her blisters and didn't dry out as fast as sneakers.

She hiked rain or shine. Her longest march in one sunny day was 28 miles, an amazing stretch in rough mountain country. When it rained, she slowed down, sang hymns, and rested often.

She told her family only that she was going for a walk. From Georgia, she sent postcards with the news that she was walking on the Appalachian Trail. But she didn't tell them that she meant to walk all the way to Maine.

At that time—1955—only about a dozen people had done this. All were men. Most people thought that hiking for months alone in the woods was not something a woman could do. Especially not an old woman. But Emma had made up her mind. She said, "I'll get there except if I break something or something busts loose. And, when I get atop Katahdin, I'll sing 'America, the Beautiful, from sea to shining sea.'"

When she had hiked 800 miles, word began to get around: a tough little grandmother was thru-hiking the "A.T." She began to find people waiting for her in trail-side towns. Reporters wrote up her story in newspapers and nicknamed her "Grandma."

She met plenty of critters. She stumbled on a huge blacksnake, so angry it was almost standing on its tail. She simply waited until the snake settled down. After a while it slid away. Many a rattlesnake shook its tail at her. One even bit at her pants. (Another good reason not to wear a skirt.)

In Connecticut a hungry bobcat circled around and "squeaked infernally" while Grandma ate lunch. "If you come too close," she told him, "I'll crack you." The bobcat backed off.

When wood mice tugged at her hair as she slept, she thought it was funny. A black bear came toward her on the trail. Grandma let loose what she called "my best holler. 'Dig!' I hollered, and he dug."

When night fell, Grandma stuffed her cloth sack full of leaves and slept on it. On cold nights she slept on stones heated in a campfire.

One evening, after a 27-mile day, Grandma was eager to sleep. She was just dozing off when she heard a flapping sound very close by. She sat up and startled a buzzard about to land on her chest. The smelly old hiker and the eater of rotten meat traded looks of surprise. Then she laughed out loud. "I knew I hadn't had a bath," she said, "but I didn't know I was THAT bad off!"

She kept on. Up and down mountains, through every kind of weather. 2100 miles. Five million steps. Finally, 146 days after getting off the bus in Georgia, she stood on Katahdin and sang "America the Beautiful," just as she said she would. She was the first woman to hike the entire Appalachian Trail, nonstop.

When she came back down, reporters saw that she had a black eye. She told how, the day before, she had fallen, twisted her ankle, broken her glasses and bruised her face. Then she gave the reporters a piece of her mind.

"I read about this Trail three years ago," she said, "and the article told about the beautiful trail, how well-marked it was.... I thought it would be a nice lark. It wasn't. There were terrible blowdowns, burnt-over areas that were never re-marked, gravel and sand washouts, weeds and brush to your neck.... Why, an Indian would die laughing his head off if he saw [that] trail. I would never have started this trip if I had known how tough it was, but I couldn't and I wouldn't quit."

That was what she said at the end of her "thru-hike." But for all her pepper, she must not have really meant it. Seventeen months later, she was back in Georgia again. At the age of sixty-nine, she set out to become the first person–man or woman–to hike the whole trail TWICE.

Why? "To see some of the things I missed the first time," she said.

But why hike so long over such rough country? reporters wanted to know. Why hike at all?

"It's hard to tell," she said. "Some people think it's crazy. But I find a restfulness—something that satisfies my nature. The woods make me feel more contented."

Another time she answered this way, "It's the thrill of being out in the forest, the peace and quiet, the beauty.... (I) slept on top (of a mountain) on a clear night, the moss just like a mattress, the moon shining and the stars so close I could almost reach out and pull them down."

One reporter guessed that she must be a long-time camper to try such things. Grandma's eyes glittered and she let out an ornery laugh. Truth be told, before trying her big hike she'd never camped out a night in her life.

Could anybody else do what she had done? "It takes more head than heels," Grandma said. "If people tell themselves to do it, they could."

Ohio found the perfect way to honor its most famous hiker. In southeastern Ohio's Hocking Hills is the state's most popular park. A six-mile footpath connects the park's two most popular sights.

Hike from Old Man's Cave to Ash Cave. You'll have walked what's known today as the Grandma Gatewood Trail.

To learn more...

Grandma Emma Gatewood's memory is maintained just the way she would have liked: a six-mile walking trail in Hocking Hills State Park is named in her honor. You can learn more about the trail by clicking on "State Parks," then "Old Man's Cave," after reaching the region's web site: <http://www.hockinghills.com/>. . Incidentally, the Gatewood Trail is part of the Buckeye Trail, a 1,200-mile path that encircles the state (and Ohio is the only state with a trail that does so). Maps and other information about the trail can be found at < http://www.ne-ohio.net/bta/>.

20

One Small Step:

Neil Armstrong

1930-

The best heroes don't show off or brag. This hero is among the world's most famous. Yet you never see him on TV. He did something great, then stepped back.

Neil Armstrong
took "one giant leap for mankind"
when he became the first man on the moon.
He and fellow astronaut Buzz Aldrin left
their footprints in the moondust.

In all its five billion lonely years, the moon had never been visited by a single living thing. But now five billion years of loneliness was ending. From Earth, the moon's neighbor, a strange little craft was drawing near. Inside were two fragile little life forms. They called themselves "men" and they called their spacecraft "the Eagle."

* * * * * * * *

July 20, 1969.

Neil Armstrong had good news for the millions of people following his adventure. The astronaut from Wapakoneta, Ohio, had set his little spacecraft safely down upon the moon. "The Eagle has landed," he told the world.

Now he had to worm out of the hatch, climb down a ladder and take a walk where no one had ever been before. He was very eager to go, but it wasn't so simple. It wasn't like opening your front door. The air pressure inside the Eagle had to be let out. It was like letting the air out of a bicycle tire. Except that it took a lot longer. Six and a half hours.

Finally, everything was ready. Armstrong and his partner Buzz Aldrin were suited up. The TV camera on the outside of the Eagle was switched on.

Neil Armstrong opened the hatch. He wriggled out and climbed slowly down the ladder. He had to be patient, careful, ready for anything. His heart was pounding fast. The sound of his own breathing seemed heavy and loud inside his helmet.

He felt clumsy in his spacesuit, but he made his way.

Back on earth, more than half a billion people around the globe watched his every move on their television sets. They saw his gloved hands clinging to the ladder, his feet finding each rung.

He reached the bottom step. The world held its breath. Then he jumped the final three and a half feet. "That's one small step for a man," he said, "One giant leap for mankind."

Later the first man on the moon admitted that he did not know what he was going to say until the last minute. It was not his style to have a speech ready. Alert, he had waited. Then, when the time was right, he found the right words. He did not say "one small step for Neil Armstrong."

A modest, small-town Ohioan, he called himself simply "a man." One of the most famous men of all time, he never tried to make people notice him.

Armstrong's booted feet settled into the dust of a silent, lifeless world. He looked about him. Everywhere there were rocks and rubble and shallow holes in the dust. These were craters, marks left by meteors that had struck the moon thousands of times over millions of years. Some were small as a basketball, others as wide as a house.

Armstrong took a step. Then another. Everything was new. Each movement and step, and every turn, was a whole adventure. But he had work to do. First, he checked one of the Eagle's footpads for problems. There were none.

Then he gathered a handful of moon dust into a plastic bag and stuffed it into a pocket. If things went wrong and they were forced to leave quickly, at least that small sample would be brought back to earth for scientists to study.

Fifteen minutes later Buzz Aldrin was at his side. "Beautiful, beautiful," he said. "Magnificent desolation."

Even standing firmly on the ground, both men felt as if they were floating. And they were tingling with excitement. Aldrin said that he was "full of goose pimples." Armstrong said they felt "like bug-eyed, five-year-old boys in a candy store."

Armstrong and Aldrin would have only two hours on the surface of the moon. They had a lot to do. They set up a TV camera sixty feet from the Eagle so that people back on Earth could watch. They took photos, picked up bits of rock and cups of sand, learned all they could. Millions viewed in wonder and delight. The two astronauts made fantastic leaps that no one can do on earth. With spacesuits on they weighed 360 pounds on earth. Here they weighed 60. They tried to jog and found that they could not quickly stop moving.

"The surface is fine and powdery," Neil Armstrong told the world, "like powdered charcoal." Standing on this strange dust, he found that he sank in "maybe an eighth of an inch." He said, "I can see the footprints of my boots...in the fine sand. It's a very soft surface...but here and there...very hard."

The two men set up tools that would radio data back to earth. One would measure future quakes and rumbles inside the moon. One was to measure the power of meteors that would smash into the moon in years to come. Yet another was to measure the sun's power.

They stuck a pole into the ground and displayed the American flag. With no air and no wind on the moon, the flag would have drooped. But a metal rod stretched out the flag for all to see.

Armstrong and Aldrin talked with President Nixon. They set in place a steel marker and Armstrong read aloud the words that were printed on it: "Here men from the planet Earth first set foot upon the moon, July 1969 A.D. We came in peace for all mankind."

His chores done at last, Armstrong took a good, long look around him. He told what he saw as millions hung on every word. "It has a very stark beauty all its own," he said slowly. "It's like much of the high desert areas of the United States...it's pretty out here."

Raw blocks of color cut starkly into each other. There were a thousand shades of gray and a hundred hues of tan, sliced here and there by the grim and utter blackness of the shadows cast by rocks.

Armstrong looked at the Eagle. It was like a giant metal spider. It gleamed silvery-gold in the hard light, its wide, round footpads pressing into the dust.

Loveliest of all was the earth. It was a perfect circle of changing greens, blues, whites and browns. It looked far larger than the moon looks from earth. The sunlight glittered on oceans and clouds and snowy plains. It was so bright that it almost hurt Armstrong's eyes. And all the while there hung the timeless backdrop of dazzling stars and deep space, black and empty.

At last it was time to go. Using a pulley and kicking up a cloud of dust, the two men lifted a 50-pound box of soil, dust and rocks into the Eagle. Back up the ladder they went, squeezed inside and shut the hatch.

The first moon walk was over.

Above them, alone in the command ship Columbia, was Mike Collins. While Armstrong and Aldrin were on the surface, Collins was circling the moon, once every 70 minutes.

Now, before leaving the moon, the two men were supposed to sleep. But they could not sleep. It was cold inside the Eagle and they had very little room. They closed their eyes, pretended to be nodding off, but it was no use. They were just too excited.

Right on schedule, Neil lifted the Eagle off the moon and made the three-and-a-half-hour trip back up into space. The Columbia would meet them sixty miles overhead.

The Eagle linked up smoothly to the command ship. Together again, the three astronauts were filled with a wild joy that had to be let out. They whooped and yelped and cheered and laughed and hollered.

Sixty hours later the Columbia splashed down safely into the ocean near Hawaii. After a few days of rest, the men were greeted by an admiring world. They were the stars of a big parade through the streets of New York City. The President gave each of them the Medal of Freedom, the highest award an American can get.

After that, the three astronauts went to 22 countries. Everywhere, crowds cheered them.

Afterwards Armstrong and his family settled into a normal life. He became a professor, and started a computer and airplane business.

In time he turned to farming. He did not "cash in" on his fame. He makes only a few speeches each year. The Ohioan knows he will always be famous because he was the first on the moon. But he also wants to live a quiet life. This is so important to him that, even when 25 years had passed after his famous moon walk, he turned away reporters. He would not let them make him a star again.

Many famous people try very hard to stay in the public eye long after they have stopped doing things that are important. Neil Armstrong is not one of those.

He has won the greatest honors the world can give. But Neil Armstrong is still what he has always been—a modest, small-town man from Ohio.

And the moon is a little less lonely.

To learn more...

A chapter about Neil Armstrong appears in *Contemporary Heroes and Heroines*, edited by Ray B. Browne (Detroit: Gale Research, 1990).

The Neil Armstrong Air and Space Museum is located beside Interstate 75 in Armstrong's hometown of Wapakoneta. Real aircraft and spacecraft, as well as a moon rock, are on display in the museum. The museum also has an exciting Astro-theater and exhibits you can operate yourself. The museum is open to the public March-November and to groups by appointment December through February; admission is charged. Call 1-800-860-0142.

The museum maintains a web site, with "lunar links" to related sites of interest, at http://www.3d-interact.com/SpaceMuseum/. The NASA Quest Project has mounted a fascinating Web site about space exploration at <http://quest.arc.nasa.gov/>.

21

Trailblazer With a Pen:

Toni Morrison
1931-

Creative people can be heroes. Writers, painters, composers make something wonderful where there was nothing before. And these things can help us see our world in fresh, new ways.

Toni Morrison,
one of America's greatest authors,
went to Hawthorne Elementary School
in Lorain. She worked as a student helper
in the public library, which now
has a reading room named in her honor.

ot long ago, in a town not far away, there lived a little African-American girl who wished her eyes were blue. What can you do when you want something? Well, she thought, you can pray.

So for two years the little girl prayed for blue eyes. But after two years her eyes were as dark as ever. She told another black girl that she was not going to believe in God anymore. Why not? her friend wanted to know. Because, she said, for two years she had prayed for blue eyes and God had not given them to her.

Her friend felt sorry. She wished she could give the girl the blue eyes she wanted so badly. But how could anyone do that? And to stop believing in God over such a thing. It made the tears want to come in her own dark eyes.

Everyone wants things they can't have, the girl thought. She herself was filled with yearnings. She wanted to do wonderful things with her life. Her dream was to be a dancer. She would dance in bright lights somewhere. She would whirl and twirl, swing and sway. The people who were watching would smile and clap their hands.

Later her dream to dance grew into another dream—to act. That was it! She would be in plays. She would speak her lines with great tenderness. She would wave her arms and work her face. She would thrill the people who were watching.

In time, she went to college and she found that she really could act in plays. But what she loved was not *the acting*. Instead, she found that she loved *the words*. So, after college, she got a job teaching English.

Soon she married. She gave birth to two sons. Then she was divorced. It was hard to be alone, to be a single mother. A teacher no more, she worked for a textbook company during the day. After work she gave all her time to her two boys.

She had wanted so much from life, but she had gotten so little. She loved her boys, but she felt sad all the time. Late at night, when the boys were asleep and the apartment was quiet, she would go to her desk and turn on the lamp. There, in the lamp's yellow pool of light, she would write. Her cares were forgotten.

Five years before this, when she was just out of college, she had joined a group of writers who met once a month. They read their writings out loud and talked about them.

The young woman didn't have much to share. She had kept a few writings from her high school and college years. She read these. But after a few meetings, she had nothing left to read.

She would have to write something new.

But what would it be? What can a person write about? Her teachers had always said to write about something you know. She asked herself, "What does Toni Morrison know?" The answer came. She knew what it was like to grow up as an African-American girl in Lorain, Ohio.

She thought about this and began to feel a thrill. It was a very good thing to know about.

She later said that Ohio was a mix "of what was ideal in this country and what was base.... Black people...came...because Ohio offered the possibility of a good life, the possibility of freedom, even though there were some terrible obstacles. Ohio...offers an escape from stereotyped black settings. It is neither plantation nor ghetto."

She began to look into the dark corners of herself and to find out what was there. Memories began to flood in upon her. One of them seemed to reach up and grab her by the neck and shake her right down to the roots of her soul.

It was what another black girl had once said to her...a funny, strange, sad thing. The girl told her that she was not going to believe in God anymore. The reason was that she had prayed for blue eyes for two years and God had not given them to her.

Toni Morrison thought hard about that girl's wish. She saw something in it that was worth writing about. She saw that her friend, like millions of black children in her time, had been made to wish that she was different than she was. She was forced to be unhappy with who she was. Toni Morrison saw how wrong and sad this was.

She dashed off a short story of a black girl who wished for blue eyes. She read it to her friends. They liked it. She felt pleased and tucked away the story. That was that...for a while.

Then, five years later, in 1967, she began to make the short story grow into a chapter book.

Later she said that she just tried to write the kind of book she knew she would like to read. It would be a book about "little black girls who were props, background ... those people were never center stage, and those people were ME."

Today it is easy for us to think of Toni Morrison writing books. She's won fame and fortune. Millions respect and admire her. In 1993 she became the first African-American to win the Nobel Prize for Literature. This is the greatest award a writer can get.

Today, it's hard to believe that, in 1967, THERE WERE NO BLACK WOMEN AUTHORS. At least none that anybody knew about. There were a few black authors who were men. Toni Morrison respected them, but she also felt that they had written for white readers. They were always telling things that black readers would already know.

T oni Morrison wanted to write a book that would use words the way the black people in her childhood had used words. She wanted to write a book that black people would know right away was for them.

She felt that, if she could do this, she could tell a story that would not be just for African-American people. It would be a story for ALL people.

A black woman trying to do such a thing? This was something new. It was as new as Edison's phonograph had been, as new as the Wright Brother's flying machine, as new as Neil Armstrong's footprint on the moon. No one else in America had ever tried to tell such a story in such a way.

She called her first book *The Bluest Eye*. It tells the story of three black girls living in Lorain, Ohio. It is a book that does not turn away from what is ugly and evil. But it is a good book to read because Toni Morrison uses words that are beautiful and tell the truth.

Writing late at night, alone in her apartment, Toni Morrison sometimes thought that no one would ever read *The Bluest Eye* until she was dead. If then. This thought did not stop her. She kept on writing.

At last *The Bluest Eye* was finished. Now she had to get it published or no one could read it. She sent *The Bluest Eye* to one publisher after another. Every time it was returned to her. No one wanted to publish it. Months passed. No one cared about her book.

She did not give up. There are many publishers. She kept sending it to one after another.

Finally, one of them said they would take a chance and publish *The Bluest Eye*. It was a big risk. No one had ever published a book like it. No one knew if people would buy it and read it. But in 1970 a publisher called Holt, Rinehart & Winston took the risk and published a strange, new book—*The Bluest Eye*. It was by an unknown young, black woman who had never published anything before.

At first, not many readers wanted to buy the book, but people who write about new books had some grand things to say about it. One wrote for the most famous newspaper in America, *The New York Times*. This person admired the new author for writing words "so precise, so faithful to speech and so charged with pain and wonder that the novel becomes poetry."

Still, no one then knew that the publishing of *The Bluest Eye* would mark the beginning of fame for one of the best writers of our time. Not even Toni Morrison herself could see then just how well-known she would become.

Her later books have been loved by readers everywhere. Readers who are black and readers who are white. Her success has gone far, far beyond the hopes of the single mother, a quiet hero alone in her apartment, writing late at night about a sad little black girl who wished her eyes were blue.

To learn more...

Every public library has the books of Toni Morrison, one of the greatest writers of our time. Her latest is *Paradise*, published in 1998. The cover story about Toni Morrison in the January 19, 1998, issue of *Time* reviews her life and work and praises *Paradise*.

Two excellent biographies written for young readers share the same title: *Toni Morrison*. Douglas Century's (Chelsea House, 1994) includes illustrations. Barbara Kramer's (Enslow, 1996) is "inspiring," says a reviewer. Linden Peach provides a brief introduction to each of her works in *Toni Morrison* (New York: St. Martin's, 1995).

A handsome and very thorough web site devoted to the author is *Anniina's Toni Morrison Page:* <http://www.luminarium.org/contemporary/tonimorrison/>.

22

"God Belongs to Me, Too!"

Baldemar Velasquez

1947-

Sometimes things are so bad that it seems nothing can be done to make them better. When things get that bad, heroes don't just complain. They get to work.

Baldemar Velasquez
leads FLOC
(Farm Labor Organizing Committeee)
on behalf of the rights of migrant workers.
Thanks to FLOC, child laborers
are no longer a common sight
in Ohio fields.

T he rat's toenails rasped on the window sill. Little Baldemar Velasquez opened his sleepy eyes. In the moonlight he could just make out the furry body and long, trailing tail. It crept onto the couch where he and his brother were trying to sleep. Their heads were at opposite ends; their feet and legs tangled together. They shared a blanket.

There was no other sound but the soft breathing of the boys' sleeping parents, brothers and sisters. Eleven in all, living in this one-room shack. They were poor. Terribly poor.

They were migrant workers. All day long they worked, picking tomatoes and cucumbers for Ohio farmers. They bent over for hours on end, stooping to pluck the vines clean, slowly filling their baskets. There was no shade and no bathrooms. Wasps and bees buzzed about their knees. Evenings were cooler, but thick with mosquitoes.

When it got too dark to work, they came back to their shacks. They cooked, ate, washed and slept, all in the same room. The weeks passed in a blur. Back and forth they went. To the fields, to the shack. Fields, shack, fields, shack. No TV. No time for baseball. No time for anything. Work, eat, sleep.

There were no days off. Cucumbers don't stop growing on weekends. They can double their size in a single summer night. They must be picked when they are small or they don't fit into pickle jars.

The rat stole onto the blanket. The brothers could feel its tiny claws on their legs. They lay still, holding their breath. Each clutched their fists onto his end of the blanket.

Suddenly they both yanked as hard as they could, pulling the blanket tight as a trampoline. The rat shot screeching into the air as the brothers roared with laughter, waking everyone. Their mother clapped her hands at the rat. The terrified creature scurried out. The mother scolded the boys in a harsh whisper. "A dormir!" she commanded. Spanish for "Go to sleep!" And soon they slept.

Baldemar had begun working in the fields when he was six. There was no choice. To eat, the whole family must work. He picked cotton in Texas, stuffing it into a bag bigger than himself. After cotton season, the family went north, looking for work.

They never knew if their pay would be fair or their living quarters clean. The men who signed them up to work often kept part of their pay. Sometimes Baldemar's parents even had to pay rent for the shacks they lived in.

Crew bosses made the pickers work hard. Baldemar heard them bawling out his parents. They shouted in English, and he could not understand the words. But he felt frozen with fear and shame.

When Baldemar was seven, the crops were spoiled by too much rain. There was no work. There was no money. Then both parents got sick. When fall came, they were too weak to go back to Texas. They were stuck in Ohio.

It was their first winter in the north. The Velasquez family huddled in an empty farmhouse. They borrowed money from a farmer to buy food. They burned firewood and coal but they were always cold. Baldemar went to school—not to learn, but to keep warm. He learned nothing because he couldn't understand the teachers. By spring the family owed the farmer so much money that they had to work all summer just to pay him back. They worked and lived like slaves.

Baldemar wondered why his family's life was so hard. "There has to be some way to do something," he thought. "Why can't anybody do anything?"

Trapped in Putnam County, the family found work on nearby farms. Baldemar kept on going to school, slowly learning English. There were other Hispanic children in his elementary school, but they all quit as the years passed. Not Baldemar. The day came when his was the only brown face in the whole class.

Sometimes the family went to church. The white Ohioans sat on one side. Baldemar's family sat with the Hispanics or "Chicanos" on the other side. The two halves of the congregation weren't friends, but they were polite.

Religion grew in Baldemar. His parents and the church gave him a belief in God and a belief that he was important. He tried to follow the teachings of Jesus and to be kind to other people.

Still, he was an outsider. Today he says, "When you're raised in a low and humble situation, you don't feel worthy. You're looked down upon. You're just a dirty Mexican. All you're good for is to harvest a crop. Then get out of town. That's what we felt like. So what do you think our vision of God was? Churches were all clean. We were a bunch of dirty migrant workers who didn't belong. We thought God must feel we weren't worthy to enter his temple.

"But one day I realized something wonderful–boom!–from the inside. This is what it was: God belongs to me, too."

His high school years were hard. "Sports were the only thing that kept me from going crazy," he says. The local farmers loved to watch him play football. "They cheered, and I was able to get some of the anger out of my system."

In college he worked for the rights of African-Americans. Then one day a black man said to him, "Baldemar, why are you here?"

Baldemar blinked and opened his mouth. Before he could answer, the man went on. "Why aren't you helping your own people?"

That question shaped his life. Baldemar went home to Putnam County. He was a man now. And he had a mission.

One person could do very little. But if hundreds, even thousands, worked together, migrant workers' lives could be better. So Baldemar went from farm to farm, telling the workers this idea. He got them to form America's first labor union for migrant workers. He signed up the first members in the very same field where the crew bosses had bawled out his parents. The workers named their new union the "Farm Labor Organizing Committee." FLOC, for short.

Some farmers didn't like the idea. Baldemar was soon arrested. But when Baldemar's story made the news, people began to realize that migrant workers had rights, too. In the years that followed, Baldemar was arrested more than thirty times, but the migrant workers' little union kept on growing.

FLOC's goals were better pay, education, food and living quarters for the migrant workers. They did not ask these things from the farmers who owned the land where the migrants worked. Instead, they aimed at the huge factories that canned and sold tomatoes and pickles.

For nine years Baldemar did his best to help FLOC reach these goals. He tried to make the factory owners understand.

"The industry was like a huge, troubled family," he says. "One part of the industry was making it hard on another part. We had to bring together the people within the industry. It was like bringing angry family members together."

Finally, when nothing else worked, FLOC decided to strike. Two thousand workers refused to pick any more crops until their demands were met. It was the largest farm strike ever. Things turned nasty. Police clubbed a FLOC lawyer, breaking his head open. The strikers were roughed up; a nun was punched in the face. Some farmers quit planting tomatoes and cucumbers. They planted corn instead. A canning factory in Leipsic, Ohio, closed—forever.

Baldemar asked all Americans to help the striking workers by refusing to buy the products of the canning factories. He led 100 workers on a 600-mile protest march from FLOC headquarters in Toledo to the headquarters of the largest canning factory in Camden, New Jersey.

People began to see that farm workers' lives were very hard. Minds were changing, little by little.

Finally, after eight years— eight years!—the Campbell Soup Company gave the striking workers what they wanted: better pay and a better life. The other canning factories soon did the same. The long strike was over. FLOC had won.

Through all FLOC's struggles, Baldemar has tried his best to be kind, even to his enemies. "If you love God with all your heart," he says, "then you will love your neighbor as yourself."

Now he has his own family. Four kids. "God put you in a family as a training ground for how to treat others," Baldemar believes. "Family is where you learn to love your neighbor."

For Baldemar Velasquez FLOC is no different. "FLOC to me is a just a larger family," he says.

Baldemar's work goes on. Many battles lie ahead. But migrant workers have better lives now, thanks to FLOC. The pay is better, the hours not so long.

And rats rasp on their window sills...no more!

To learn more...

Two fine books for young readers about the plight of migrant farm workers are: *Voices from the Field: Children of Migrant Farmworkers Tell Their Stories*, by S. Beth Atkin (New York: Little, Brown, 1993) and *Migrant Farm Workers: the Temporary People*, by Linda Jacobs Altman (Danbury, Conn.: Franklin Watts, 1994).

In 1996 the Public Broadcast System aired a four-part series entitled *Chicano: the History of the Mexican-American Civil Rights Movement*. A Web site for the series contains a great deal of information, including a useful list of print resources for students: <http://www.pbs.org/chicano/>.

The Farm Labor Organizing Committee headquarters and Baldemar Velasquez's office are in Toledo; tel. (419) 243-3456.

The Maneuver Man:

Henry Heimlich M.D.
1920-

A lifeguard or firefighter who saves a life is a hero. Meet a man who has saved more lives than all the lifeguards and firefighters put together. More than anyone else alive.

Henry Heimlich,
whose ideas have saved
thousands of lives,
grew up in an age when Jews
sometimes were the victims of bias.
Today Dr. Heimlich's name is
honored around the world.

oung Dr. Heimlich peered into the darkness. A little Chinese man staggered toward him. He was carrying something heavy, so heavy that he could hardly walk. No one knew how many miles of desert sand he had crossed. At last he reached the doctor's doorway. He eased his burden to the ground. Stiffly, yet tenderly. To him it was, in all the world, the most precious thing. It was...his daughter.

The girl was near death. Her stomach was sticking out terribly. Something was pressing on her insides. She hadn't eaten for many days. But her father heard of an American doctor far across the desert. He had no car, no horse. So he carried her.

She needed water but could not drink. Dr. Heimlich gave her a shot of salt water. What was wrong with her? He didn't know. He could not cut into her belly at night because there were no electric lights. Only candles.

In the morning she was a little better. What to do? He was the only doctor there, deep in the Gobi Desert of Inner Mongolia. He was part of a top-secret team far behind enemy lines. It was 1945, and the world was at war.

Henry Heimlich was just twenty-four years old. He, too, had come a very long way. As a young Jewish man he had struggled with what to do with his life. In the 1930s many jobs were closed to Jews. Even training to become a doctor was hard. Few Jews were accepted into medical schools.

Luckily, Heimlich was accepted into the Cornell Medical College in New York City. After that he joined the U.S. Navy and worked in its hospitals. Then one day he was ordered to report to the Chief of Naval Operations in Washington, D.C.

Dr. Heimlich was told to go to China and join a team on a long, risky mission. He took a ship to India, where he met his other teammates.

They boarded a plane to fly over the Himalayas, the world's tallest mountains. There was oxygen only for the pilots. As the plane went higher, the air grew thinner. All but the pilots passed out. They came to only when the plane was over the mountains and down the other side.

Then the young doctor crossed hundreds of miles of scrub grass and hard, dry, brown dirt. At last they reached the Gobi Desert. Pure white sand in all directions. Very hot by day, very cold at night.

There was in those parts a Chinese general with an army of almost a hundred thousand men. Dr. Heimlich's job was to help keep this leader on the Americans' side in the war against the Japanese. He decided to do this by training a medical staff for the general.

But he could also treat the Chinese people–if they would let him. At first they did not trust him. They had never seen Americans before and they called them "devils." Most were dressed in ragged jackets and fur caps pulled down over their ears. There were Mongols, too, with pointed hats. Six feet tall, Hank seemed like a giant to the Chinese. His pale white face and American clothes were strange to them.

Some of the Chinese were sick, but they trusted only their own medical customs. Their country was five thousand years old and they knew many things. They knew how to use needles and herbs to treat illness. Why trust an American doctor?

Then came the man, carrying his daughter. Everyone knew she was going to die. Nothing could save her. But should the young doctor try?

It would be a big risk. What if he opened her belly and she died? The Chinese would never trust an American after that. Perhaps the general and his whole army would then join the Japanese. It was a tough call. But Dr. Heimlich knew he had to try.

He boiled water to clean his tools and numbed the girl with an injection. He pulled the sheets away from her belly and made a clean, steady cut. It sprayed like a water balloon. It was shocking, but Dr. Heimlich laughed with joy.

It was just a simple sickness! Bad, but easy to treat. He knew what to do. The girl was soon saved.

After a few days, the father took his daughter home. Word of her recovery spread. Soon hundreds were coming to the American doctor.

But, as any doctor finds, he could not save them all. "A Chinese soldier got shot in the chest during training," Dr. Heimlich recalls. "The first night I just put on a bandage because the light was really bad. I had never opened a chest before. By morning he was near death." He tried to sew the man's wound shut, "but closing it was impossible. So much torn tissue. The patient died.... I always felt guilty. Was there anything else I could have done?"

This question later led Dr. Heimlich to invent the "Heimlich Chest Drain Valve." What is it? "Basically, you put a tube into the chest through the wound, and the tube leads to the valve. Air, blood and fluid can come out, but nothing can go in, so the lung keeps working."

Before the Heimlich Chest Valve, people who had been shot or stabbed in the chest died. Always. The valve saved thousands of lives during the Vietnam War. Once, much later, a doctor told Dr. Heimlich, "I was on Hill 881 in Vietnam. Thirty-four of my men were shot in the chest and thirty-two got off alive because of the Heimlich valve."

Today America is friends with Vietnam again partly because of Dr. Heimlich. A few years ago Dr. Heimlich went to Viet Nam to try to build a friendship between the two countries. Again and again he was told, "Everyone in Vietnam knows your name. Your valve saved thousands of our people."

"I was surprised," he says now. "At the beginning of every meeting, someone would say, almost like a prayer, 'Dr. Heimlich will live in the hearts of the Vietnamese people forever.' When I first heard this, I burst out crying. I'm so lucky that I should be someone who had the idea for that invention, which is a very simple thing."

Dr. Heimlich is a Cincinnati doctor whose name has become known around the world. His name is the most famous doctor's name of our time. "It's a name known for doing good things," he says. "I feel I have had such a good life that I owe the world something in return. I feel I must use this name to bring about a caring world. That's my main goal in life at this time."

Henry Heimlich has many medical inventions to his credit. He has saved more lives than anyone else alive. Today the valve alone saves the lives of about 250,000 people each year. It saves far more lives than the better known Heimlich Maneuver.

(Do you know the Heimlich Maneuver? When someone is choking, you hug them from behind, one hand pressing the other fist hard between their bellybutton and ribs. A few quick pushes up, and the food flies out of their throat. They're saved. The Heimlich Maneuver also gets the water out of drowning people's lungs. It even stops asthma attacks.)

"Helping and caring for people makes you a hero." Dr. Heimlich wants kids to know this. "Kids owe all other people, just for being on this earth. They owe all the good that they can do."

"The guy who makes millions of dollars is not a hero. I don't say he's bad or good–but the true hero is the one who brings health and support to people.

And the Chinese father? Dr. Heimlich saw him once more. A few weeks after his daughter was saved, the father came back with a cow on a rope.

"Think how much his cow meant to this poor man," Dr. Heimlich says. "It was almost everything he had. He badly needed that cow for milk and to pull his plow through the fields. Someday the cow would be meat for him and for his family. But he had come to give me his cow as a present, to thank me for saving his daughter."

"I could not take it. Yet I knew that if I turned down his gift, he would feel ashamed for the rest of his life. So I thanked him. I said, 'Thank you so much. You have given me a wonderful gift. But now I have a problem. I can't take care of my fine cow here. Will you help me? Will you please keep my cow and take good care of her for me?

"The man smiled and bowed and said yes. Then, tugging the cow behind him, he left, full of joy because he could do this for me."

To learn more...

Your library may have a copy *of Dr. Heimlich's Home Guide to Emergency Medical Situations* (New York: Simon & Schuster, 1980). It tells the story of how Dr. Heimlich's famous "maneuver" to save choking victims came about. It, along with many other life-saving methods that anyone can learn, is explained in an easy-to-understand way.

Many first-aid classes teach the Heimlich Maneuver. Illustrated charts showing how to use the Heimlich Maneuver for both choking and drowning victims are available from the Heimlich Institute Foundation, Inc., P.O. Box 8858, Cincinnati, OH 45208. (Restaurants and cafeterias everywhere post the chart in their kitchens.)

How to recognize symptoms of choking, and how to perform the Heimlich Maneuver on both adults and children, is explained in the web site of the Arnot Ogden Medical Center of Elmira, N.Y.: <http://www.aomc.org>. Scroll down on the welcome page and click on "Search" (marked by the Dalmatian dog) to find the search tool; then choose the Arnot Ogden Archive and type in "Heimlich Maneuver."

Index

Andrews, James J. 41, 43

Andrews' Raiders. 40-44

Appalachian Trail 113-116

Armstrong, Neil 117-122

Bickerdyke, Mary Ann 45-50

Boone, Daniel 10, 12

Buffalo Bill 85

Bulgaria 76-80

Chapman, John 3-8

China 137-138, 140

Cincinnati, OH 35-38, 66, 139

Civil War 38, 41, 46-47, 52-54

Cleveland, OH 88, 90-92

Clyde, OH 106

Columbus,OH 65

Congressional Medal of Honor 40, 44, 106, 110

Dayton, OH 72

Eagle (landing craft) 119

Edison, Thomas A. 57-62

Electricity 62, 68

Farm Labor Organizing Committee 130, 133-134

Galesburg, IL 46, 47

Gatewood, Emma 111-116

General (locomotive) 41

Georgetown, OH 53

Georgia 41

Girard, OH 95

Grant, Ulysses S. 48, 51-56

Granville, OH 65

Green Springs, OH 107

Harrison, William Henry 17-20, 23, 26

Hauser, Elizabeth 93-98

Hayes, Rutherford B. 61

Heimlich Maneuver 139

Heimlich, Dr. Henry 135-140

Hitler, Adolph 101, 103-104

Hunter, Jane Edna 87-92

Indians 6-7, 11-14, 15-20

"Johnny Appleseed" 3-8

Kenton, Simon 9-14

Lake Erie, Battle of 22-26
Lincoln, Abraham 38, 80
MacGahan, Januarius 75-80
Mansfield, OH 4, 8
Medal of Honor 40, 44, 106, 110
Mercerville, OH 113
migrant workers 131-134
Morrison, Toni 123-128
Mount Vernon, OH 8
New Lexington, OH 76
Niagara 22, 24-26
Nobel Prize 127
Oakley, Annie 81-86
Olympics 100, 101-104
Owens, Jesse 99-104
"Parade in the Rain" 97-98
Parker, John 27-32
Parrott, Jacob 39-44
Perry, Oliver Hazard 21-26
Phillis Wheatley Association 88, 91-92
Phonograph 61
Rankin, Rev. John & Jean 29, 32, 36
Revolutionary War 5
Ripley, OH 28-28, 36
Russia 78, 79
Sherman, William T. 50
Stowe, Harriet Beecher 33-38
Suffragettes 95
Taft, William Howard 70, 74
Tecumseh 12
Tecumseh 15-20
Turkey 78, 79
Twain, Mark 55
Uncle Tom's Cabin 37-38
Underground Railroad 28, 29, 32, 36
Velasquez, Baldemar 129-134
Wapokaneta, OH 119, 121
War of 1812 .... 7-8, 20, 23
Woods, Granville 63-68
World War II 108-110, 137
Wright, Katherine 69-74
Wright, Orville 69-74
Wright, Wilbur 69-74
Young, Rodger 105-110

The Author

Rick Sowash has always believed that "where you are is who you are." Rick Sowash has lived all his life in Ohio and has shaped his life's work from his knowledge of the state. As a boy he was inspired by his grandfather to gather up Ohio history, geography and folklore. As an adult he has shaped what he has learned into stories, books and musical compositions.

A veteran storyteller and long recognized as "the master of the Tall Tale," Rick has logged thousands of performances across the country. His work in this genre grew into his highly successful book of Ohio tall tales, *Ripsnorting Whoppers! Humor from America's Heartland.*

Many of the 160 works of classical music he has composed have been published, recorded, broadcast and performed around the world. His new *Quintet for Clarinet and Strings* was premiered in Paris in 1996. Rick was there to introduce the piece to the audience and make a speech (in French).

He has been a full-time, self-employed writer, humorist and composer since 1990. Before that he worked as a county commissioner, an arts administrator. A radio broadcaster, an innkeeper and a church musician. Rick lives in Cincinnati with his wife of 26 years and their two children, 13 and 16.

The Artist

The painting on the cover and the many excerpts from it throughout the book are by Marcia Muth. Though she now lives in Santa Fe, New Mexico, Marcia lived in Ohio at one time. Born in 1919 in Fort Wayne, Indiana (Johnny Appleseed's burial place, by the way), she was educated at the University of Michigan. A librarian, she has worked in public and university libraries in Ohio, Indiana, Michigan and New Mexico. In 1967 she moved to New Mexico. A self-taught folk artist, she started painting in 1974. Most of her pictures reflect her Midwestern background. Her work is in corporate, private and museum collections.

The Designer

This book's graphic design, as well as the typesetting and image preparation, are the work of Paul Obringer, creative director of UniGraphics. A native Ohioan from Fort Recovery, Paul received his Bachelor of Fine Arts degree from Bowling Green State University. His work has appeared in *Print* magazine and has won numerous design awards. UniGraphics is the creative design and service bureau of Bowling Green State University.

Picture Credits

The Publisher appreciates the assistance of many sources in illustrating *Heroes of Ohio*. In all cases cited below, use was by permission.

Cover painting, frontispiece and illustrations on chapter title pages by Marcia Muth; copyright Gabriel's Horn Publishing Co.

Photographs of Rick Sowash © by Joseph Galli, Cincinnati.
Photograph of Marcia Muth by Carolyn Wright, Santa Fe, NM.
Photograph of Paul Obringer by James Bissland.

Page 4: upper left, picture from Howe's *Historical Collections of Ohio* (1896 edition), loaned by James Bissland; right, Ohio Historical Society; bottom, Mansfield/Richland County Public Library. Page 10: upper right, Ohio Historical Society; center, sculpture by Mike Major of Urbana; bottom, picture provided through the courtesy of Ray Crain. Page 16: top and bottom, Ohio Historical Society; center, The Scioto Society, Inc., Chillicothe.
Page 22: top, Ohio Historical Society; center left, Erie Maritime Museum, Erie, Pennsylvania; painting by Gilbert Stuart. Page 28: top, *Historical Collections of Ohio*, loaned by James Bissland; center and bottom, Ohio Historical Society. Page 34: top, Ohio Historical Society; center, Corbis-Bettmann; bottom, Cleveland Public Library.
Page 40: all, Wood County Public Library, Bowling Green. Page 46: center, Galesburg, Illinois, Public Library; bottom, Western Reserve Historical Society. Page 52: all from Ohio Historical Society. Page 58: top right, James Bissland; center, Corbis-Bettmann; bottom, Cleveland Public Library. Page 64: top, Anacostia Museum, Smithsonian Institution; bottom, Ohio Historical Society. Page 70: top, National Air and Space Museum, Smithsonian Institution; bottom, Carillon Historical Park, Dayton. Page 76: top, center, Ohio Historical Society; bottom, James Bissland. Page 82: top, Garst Museum, Greenville; bottom, Ohio Historical Society. Page 88: upper left, James Bissland; right, Western Reserve Historical Society; bottom, Cleveland Public Library. Page 94: upper left, The Upton Association; upper right and bottom, Western Reserve Historical Society.
Page 100: top, Ohio Historical Society; bottom, Corbis-Bettmann. Page 106: top and right, Corbis-Bettmann; lower left, James Bissland. Page 112: all from Appalachian Trail Conference. Page 118: all from NASA. Page 124: top, James Bissland; bottom, © 1997 Timothy Greenfield-Sanders, courtesy of Random House, Inc. Page 130: bottom left, Barbara Vogel; all others courtesy of Farm Labor Organizing Committee. Page 136: all from The Heimlich Institute, Cincinnati.

Ripsnorting Whoppers!
Humor from America's Heartland

If you've enjoyed this book by Rick Sowash, you'll love another by the same author: *Ripsnorting Whoppers! Humor from America's Heartland.* It's been called "a treasury of witty, wise and wonderful Americana, masterfully told."

These are yarns in the American tradition of tall tales: hilarious stories of incredible animals and astounding people from rural Ohio. Here you'll meet Cy Gatton, whose storytelling skill at an early age had the most astonishing effect. You'll visit a mysterious place called Wildcat Hollow and find out what happened there one summer day. You'll see the fastest hunting dog in the world come to life. And you'll learn about the day the preacher lost his false teeth (and how they were found!).

All the stories are told only the way the Master of the Tall Tale—Rick Sowash—can tell them. They're available in book form (softcover and hardcover), audio cassette, and video cassette (60 minutes each). As one reader observed, "You'll laugh and laugh."

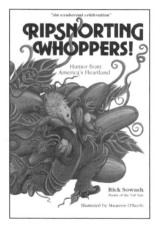

To order, call Gabriel's Horn Publishing Co., Inc., at

1-800-235-4676

see our web site
www.hornbooks.com

or use the order form at the end of this book.

To order

books and tapes by Rick Sowash,
use order form on other side

Order Form for Books and Tapes By Rick Sowash
This form may be copied

If the Rick Sowash items you want aren't available at your favorite store, you may order them directly from the publisher and receive fast service. Telephone 1-800-235-4676 , e-mail or mail form and payment to:

Gabriel's Horn Publishing Co., Inc.
Department H
P.O. Box 141
Bowling Green, OH 43402

Quantity	Title and Version	Price each	Total
_____	HEROES OF OHIO (softcover)	$11.95	$_____
_____	HEROES OF OHIO (hardcover)	$19.95	$_____
_____	RIPSNORTING WHOPPERS! (soft)	$11.95	$_____
_____	RIPSNORTING WHOPPERS! (hard)	$19.95	$_____
_____	RIPSNORTING WHOPPERS! (audio)	$9.95	$_____
_____	RIPSNORTING WHOPPERS! (video)	$24.95	$_____
	Ohio residents add 6% tax.		$_____
	UPS SHIPPING: $3.50 first item, 50¢ each thereafter.		$_____
	TOTAL AMOUNT ENCLOSED *Check or MasterCard / VISA acceptable.*		$_____

Name _____

Street address (no P.O. boxes) _____

City_____ State_____ ZIP_____

Card no._____ Expires _____

QUESTIONS? E-mail gabriel@hornbooks.com or call 1-800-235-4676.